A Brief History of N

On July 20, 1899, the newsboys of New York City [illegible] Joseph Pulitzer's *New York World* and William Randolph Hearst's *New York Journal* to protest the higher prices they were charged for newspapers. Their strike, which lasted nearly two weeks before it was resolved through a historic compromise, was a harbinger for child labor reforms in the 20th century.

To pay tribute to the newsboys' story, The Walt Disney Company premiered *Newsies* on April 10, 1992. The live-action musical feature film was written by Bob Tzudiker and Noni White, and directed by Kenny Ortega, with songs by Alan Menken and Jack Feldman. After receiving generally poor reviews, the movie quickly disappeared from theaters.

On October 14, 1992, Disney released *Newsies* on VHS and Beta home video. The movie premiered on the Disney Channel as part of a "Free Spring Preview" on March 28, 1993. In the following years, home viewing and the advent of the Internet spawned a passionate fan base.

Due to overwhelming requests to license a live-stage version of *Newsies*, Disney Theatrical Productions put the title into development. Harvey Fierstein joined the project as book writer in 2009, and Menken and Feldman complemented their original film score with several new songs. Developmental readings took place in New York City in May and December of 2010.

On September 25, 2011, a test production of *Newsies: The Musical* opened at Paper Mill Playhouse in Millburn, New Jersey; it was directed by Jeff Calhoun and choreographed by Christopher Gattelli. Positive critical and "Fansie" responses opened unexpected doors.

Newsies began previews of a limited Broadway run at the Nederlander Theatre on March 15, 2012, and opened on March 29. After the show sold out its initial 12 weeks and a 10-week extension, Disney announced an open-ended run on May 16, 2012. The musical earned eight 2012 Tony Award nominations and won for Best Original Score and Best Choreography.

Newsies celebrated its first anniversary on March 29, 2013, crossed the 500-performance mark on June 8, 2013, and continues to thrill audiences eight times a week at the Nederlander Theatre.

NEW

SIES

STORIES OF THE UNLIKELY BROADWAY HIT

Edited by KEN CERNIGLIA

CONTENTS

6 Foreword

7 From the Editor

8 An Unlikely Journey to Broadway

SECTION A 11 **The Newsboys' Strike of 1899**
Historical foundations of *Newsies*

SECTION B 25 **Depicting a Fine Life on Film**
The creation and reception of the movie

SECTION C 41 **Seizing the Demand**
Making a stage musical for fans

SECTION D 51 **Let's Watch What Happens**
A production test at Paper Mill Playhouse

SECTION E 93 **Kings of New York**
Newsies comes to the Great White Way

SECTION F 117 **Carrying That Banner**
Supporting an extended Broadway run

SECTION G 147 **The World Knows**
Final reflections from the *Newsies* family

OPPOSITE: Jeremy Jordan as Jack Kelly

Foreword

Thomas Schumacher
producer and president
Disney Theatrical Group (DTG)

When *Newsies* hit the screen in 1992, the rebirth of the film musical was going on over at Disney Feature Animation, where I was working at the time, and we saw this live-action film as almost a spillover of that movement. What became clear is that audiences were happy to embrace singing mermaids and flying carpets in the movie theater, but dancing newsboys . . . maybe not so much.

My earliest true sense of the potential of *Newsies* came not from production (because that was not in my sphere of activity, though it involved a number of my friends and colleagues), but rather from the way my young nephew Michael was obsessed with it and wanted the movie poster to hang over his bed. As a dedicated uncle with access to the marketing department, I promptly accommodated his request. Michael's passion for the story of young men taking charge of their lives and changing the course of history in some ways prophesied how the film made its way to the stage.

It sounds nutty, especially since Disney Theatrical Productions had not yet taken flight, but all of the key players in *Newsies*' stage saga were circling Feature Animation even as the film reels were spinning at the premiere. *Newsies* authors Bob Tzudiker and Noni White were now in the writers' room on *The Lion King*. Harvey Fierstein had not yet given voice to Yao in *Mulan*, but he was writing an animated version of *The Snow Queen*, a tale that bounced around the studio from Walt's day all the way to the fall of 2013, with the release of *Frozen*. Alan Menken, who was already a legend because of *The Little Mermaid*, *Beauty and the Beast*, and *Aladdin*, now had a new lyric partner, Jack Feldman, who had worked on *Oliver & Company* back in 1988.

I am often asked what makes one story or another appropriate for Broadway. In a business where 75% of the shows that open do not recoup their initial investment, everyone is always looking for a recipe. There is none, but there are clues. Like the vast majority of Broadway hits, *Newsies* is based on preexisting material—the film and the historical event that inspired it. *Newsies* is also a musical, and onstage, these characters expressing themselves through song and dance can seem reasonable: public demonstrations are "dances," and making speeches to rally a group is like singing. Then comes perhaps the most elusive element of all, timing.

People who had grown up with the film, who were inspired by its David-and-Goliath story and its optimism that the status quo can be overturned by voices united, wanted to see it onstage and they told us so. Not just my nephew (who not ironically is a labor leader today), but also students in high schools and colleges throughout the country, who had come to love *Newsies* through the magic of home video, kept asking for the stage version of their beloved story. There was a calling. And like the story of the newsboys themselves, this show, based on a footnote of history and a flop film, became an unlikely success onstage.

All good stories have heroes. This one has several without whom *Newsies* would simply not have happened. Principal among them are Bob Tzudiker and Noni White, who set the path; Harvey Fierstein, who got us out of the woods; Alan Menken and Jack Feldman, who gave it a voice; Jeff Calhoun and Christopher Gattelli, who staged it with deftness and heart; Chris Montan, who touches everything musical; and Steve Fickinger, who kept the flame alive through years of development when lesser teams would have split apart at the seams.

From the Editor

Ken Cerniglia
dramaturg and literary manager, DTG

This volume constitutes the eighth book to document the creation and production of a Disney Broadway show, beginning in 1995 with Donald Frantz's *Beauty and the Beast: A Celebration of the Broadway Musical*. Julie Taymor followed with *The Lion King: From Pride Rock to Broadway* (with Alexis Greene), then award-winning writer Michael Lassell commanded the pen for a series of wonderful books that tracked Disney's productions in the first decade of the new millennium: *Elton John and Tim Rice's AIDA: The Making of the Broadway Musical*, *Tarzan: The Broadway Adventure*, *Mary Poppins: Anything Can Happen if You Let It* (with Brian Sibley), and *The Little Mermaid: From the Deep Blue Sea to the Great White Way*.

As *Newsies* was making its way to the Nederlander Theatre in early 2012, Disney's first play, *Peter and the Starcatcher*, also found a home on Broadway thanks to a partnership with outside producers. For that show, Wendy Lefkon (editorial director for Disney Editions) agreed to publish Rick Elice's entire script, and I edited annotations by the creative team and included deleted scenes and a production history. The book was beautifully designed by Clark Wakabayashi of Welcome Enterprises and featured stunning production

Brendon Stimson

photography by Deen Van Meer.

As soon as we finished that book, *Newsies* announced its conversion from a limited to an open-ended Broadway run, so it was time to turn our documentary attention to this phenomenon of unique history, energy, and appeal. Although I had the privilege of working as a dramaturg on the show since its early days and had thus witnessed much of its development firsthand, it seemed to me that the story of *Newsies* coming to Broadway was so remarkable, so unlikely, that there was no one right way to tell it. So, with the blessing of Tom Schumacher (and Wendy and Clark), we issued an open invitation to the entire creative team, cast, crew, staff, and audience (the "Fansies") to submit stories in their own words for inclusion in this book. This happened right around the first anniversary of *Newsies* at the Nederlander Theatre, so this has become a yearbook of sorts. The stories include both written submissions and edited interviews.

Many of my colleagues at Disney Theatrical Group eagerly stepped up to help conceive and corral this massive project, including Jane Abramson, Caley Beretta, Elizabeth Boulger, Whitney Britt, Eduardo Castro, Michael Deicas, Adam Dworkin, Greg Josken, Colleen McCormack, Lisa Mitchell, Brendan Padgett, David Scott, Seth Stuhl, Anji Limón Taylor, and Peter Tulba. To them, and to everyone who volunteered stories (and photos, drawings, stats, and scraps) for inclusion in these pages, I am sincerely grateful.

An Unlikely Journey to Broadway

Steve Fickinger

vice president of creative development, DTG

Theater is a world that doesn't change very much; the curtain goes up, and actors speak the speech, sing, dance, and try to tell the audience a story that will make them laugh, make them cry, make them think, and touch their hearts. The "business of the business," however, does change with the tides. Time was when in order for a show to enter the public consciousness and join the pantheon of beloved stage titles, there was a crucial stop: Broadway. And if you were lucky enough to make it to Broadway, then you better be a hit. That time, arguably, has passed. Nowadays, when you take a known or beloved property and transfer it to the stage, it can become a success without ever taking residence on the Great White Way. Disney's own *High School Musical: On Stage* enjoyed an astonishing global embrace but never touched down in Manhattan.

Perhaps some of our most recognizable and well-loved titles are from the Disney catalog. To tap into that potential, Disney decided to create a series of Broadway-caliber shows that would enter the licensing catalog without ever running the Broadway gauntlet. These shows would be created to be licensed and produced by professional theaters, amateur theaters, schools, and community groups. Disney keeps track of things—a lot of things—well . . . everything. One of the lists generated on an annual basis is the top-requested titles for stage adaptations. It can be viewed as sort of a "wish list" of shows that people hope to perform, and can act as a barometer of the appeal of possible stage titles. Year after year, one title made its appearance either at the top or near the top of the list: *Newsies*. (As for the other titles, feel free to turn your guesses into a parlor game—we're not telling!)

Now, the fortunes of this film in its initial release are subjects of legend and lore, and a tale best told by others. All that remains certain is that thanks to the Disney Channel and home video, *Newsies* spawned a generation of die-hard acolytes. So the people spoke and their pleas were heard; a stage adaptation—for licensing only—went into development in 2006. The original creative team was and is in such a high level of demand that getting the participants to the table to have the first discussion took one whole year. The path of developing a show is usually long, circuitous, and a whole different story altogether. Life changes, stuff happens, people come, people go, ideas are embraced and discarded, hopes are raised, and dreams are dashed. There is no surefire formula, and as the old saying goes, "If it were easy, everyone would do it."

So let's fast-forward through countless table reads, changes in the creative team, two professional readings, and we land ourselves in December 2010. A fairly successful second reading took place, and now it was time to take the plunge—time to mount a test, or "pilot" production. A deal was brokered with Mark Hoebee and the fantastic people at Paper Mill Playhouse in Millburn, New Jersey, to mount a co-production in the fall of 2011 (yes, 10 months later—see why these things take so long?). After a painstaking search, a top-tier team of director Jeff Calhoun, choreographer Chris Gattelli, and an astonishingly talented and resourceful group of designers came together to bring this stage reinvention to life. Let's remember—the goal was to put the stage adaptation on its feet, work out the kinks, and then place it into the licensing catalog. If lightning struck, then perhaps a small tour.

Outside the Nederlander Theatre on West 41st Street, New York City

One important question remained: just how many of these hard-core *Newsies* fans were actually out there? 50? 500? 5,000? Could the uninitiated be converted? Was the title alone enough to fill the theater for the Paper Mill run? Would there be rioting in the streets of Millburn when the "Fansies" (as the diehards are known) caught wind of the changes made during transfer from screen to stage? Well, the day of reckoning came as it always must, and the verdict was in: the audience didn't like it . . . they loved it! There was jubilation in the streets (well, at least in the halls of Disney Theatrical) as the audience came from far and wide, lavished their love, and Glory Hallelujah, the critics followed suit. So the question on everybody's lips was: "To go to Broadway, or not to go?"

Let's pause for a moment to share an anecdote. There's nothing more thrilling than watching a professional at the top of her craft make a call that's a game-changer. There came a moment in the crunching of the budget numbers for Paper Mill that a hard fact couldn't be ignored: the cost of the set was "just too damn high." That's when peerless production executive Anne Quart had a stroke of genius: instead of cutting the budget for the set, why not spend a bit more and create a set that could be repurposed after Paper Mill for that possible small tour or to rent to licensed productions? This idea would have a profound effect on the future plans for *Newsies*.

At the end of the Paper Mill run, after much debate, it was decided that a limited Broadway run of *Newsies* would be mounted in the spring/summer of 2012. This 12-week run would give the show a Broadway imprimatur and help raise its fortunes as a licensed title. And thanks to Anne's savvy, the set from Paper Mill could be easily moved to the Nederlander Theatre, vastly lowering the cost of a Broadway transfer. Rehearsals began in February 2012, and previews started a short four weeks later. All the usual questions hung in the air. Was Paper Mill a fluke? Would audiences pay the necessarily higher Broadway ticket price? Could the Fansie heat really sustain a summerlong run?

Newsies opened on Broadway on March 29, 2012, to a wild and warm reception and continues to play to packed houses. At this moment, there's no end in sight. So, dreams come true, the "ugly duckling" just might be a swan, and for the thousands of people who have seen, will see, or perhaps even perform this show, it is indeed a "fine life, carrying the banner."

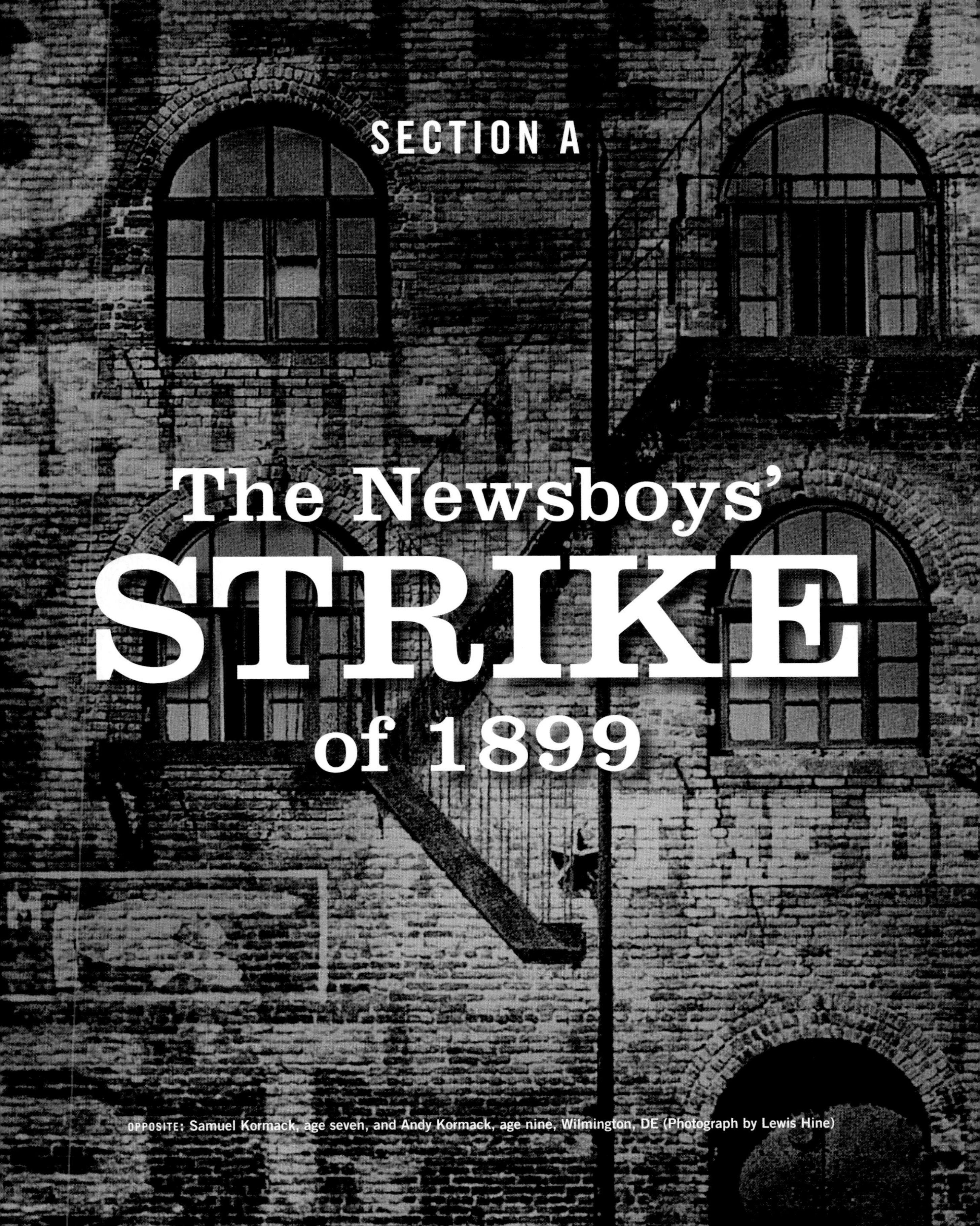

SECTION A

The Newsboys' STRIKE of 1899

OPPOSITE: Samuel Kormack, age seven, and Andy Kormack, age nine, Wilmington, DE (Photograph by Lewis Hine)

Lower Manhattan, New York City, c. 1900
STEWART BUILDING
EMIGRANT INDUS. SAVINGS BANK
HALL OF RECORDS
MUNICIPAL BUILDING
COURT HOUSE
CITY COURT
CITY HALL
POST OFFICE
PULITZER BUILDING
TRIBUNE BUILDING
POTTER BUILDING
TRACT HOUSE
TEMPLE COURT
VANDERBILT BUILDING
BROOKLYN BRIDGE

Finding Dramatic Inspiration in a Footnote of History

Bob Tzudiker
co-screenwriter, *Newsies* (1992)

OPPOSITE: The inset of this map of lower Manhattan in the early 1900s shows the square where City Hall is located. Across Park Row stood the headquarters of Joseph Pulitzer's *The World.* ABOVE: Newsboys selling near the Brooklyn Bridge, New York (Lewis Hine)

> "There were dozens and dozens of ways for enterprising 11- to 15-year-olds to make money in the early 20th-century cities. Of them all, the most accessible and most fun was selling newspapers."
>
> — **DAVID NASAW, *Children of the City: At Work & at Play***

Looking back to the birth of *Newsies* could make me feel old. And I'm not. I'm really not. But we (Noni White, my wife and partner, and I) started working on the movie before the Internet was in common use, back in the days of faxing and having to physically go to libraries to find physical books. Out of curiosity, I just did a Web search for the newsie strike and found over 120,000 hits in .24 seconds, no doubt some of it material I have never seen despite many weeks of research. I first came across the idea of the strike in 1985 when reading *The New York Times*—quaint in itself, although I still read the newspaper every day. A book review of David Nasaw's wonderful *Children of the City*, about the lives of urban American children at the turn of the 20th century, mentioned that he had unearthed a film-worthy tale of the New York Newsboys' Strike of 1899. Based on that one paragraph about one chapter, I made a note in my list of ideas and set it aside.

A couple of years passed. Noni and I both continued acting, which is a great part-time job if you want lots of free time to write and can keep your expenses low. I have no idea why I thought I was a writer, with no training, no mentor, no outside encouragement. But I'd had no training as an actor, either (although I think it showed in my film work), and here I was making a living at it. Noni and I finished our first screenplay on spec, a romantic comedy which did not sell (at the time) but was well received. We found a new writing agent, Caren Bohrman, who asked us to develop ideas to pitch. The newsie strike was one of those ideas we brought her. "Which one are you most passionate about?" Caren asked. "*Newsies*," we replied instantly, "but it's a period piece with kids and it gets violent. No studio will touch it. And our only writing sample is a comedy."

Hyman, age six, Lawrence, MA (Lewis Hine)

She didn't disagree. She just shrugged and told us to pitch what we were most passionate about.

We set about learning everything we could about the newsboys' strike of 1899. My parents lived outside Washington, D.C., at the time, so we asked them to hit the Library of Congress. A couple of weeks later we received a box full of copies of newspapers from the day. I couldn't find Dr. Nasaw's book (no Amazon), but my sister lived in Berkeley, California, where good bookstores abound. She found a used copy (perfect for our budget) and sent it down to L.A.

Research is eternally seductive, especially with so rich a subject. But history has to be set aside at some point; we had to design a story. Our first choice was of the antagonist. Hearst or Pulitzer? We picked Pulitzer simply because Hearst had been "taken" by Orson Welles for *Citizen Kane*. Also, Pulitzer would have been a natural ally of the newsies, and that conflict between his business and his politics was interesting to us. But little of that internal conflict survived the ruthless compression of film story.

I had lived in Santa Fe, New Mexico, so we chose that as Jack's goal, with all the romance and adventure that comes with that city's name. Several newsie leaders had been accused of betraying the cause, which inspired us to invent Jack, who would discover, lose, and redeem himself. We invented David as the moral center. For a love interest, we had a girl newsie, Charlie, who dressed like a boy and had an unrequited crush on Jack. In our original ending, Jack hops the train to Santa Fe with Charlie, but the budget would not allow a train, and subsequent changes replaced Charlie with David's sister anyway.

Anyone who takes 100% credit for a film is a liar. Screenwriter Dalton Trumbo observed that the more money required

"Hawking papers was fun, but it was also work that required physical exertion and no small amount of careful planning. Children who expected to earn decent money on the streets had to apply themselves to mastering the economics of their trade."

— DAVID NASAW

to produce a work of art, the less control any one person has over the final product. Films, as the most expensive art form, offer the least control to any one person. This includes writers, directors, and studio chiefs. (If you want control, Trumbo advised, write a pamphlet.) When we write a screenplay, we do not expect the resulting film to completely reflect our creation. The differences could be minor, or our original intent can be completely altered. We count ourselves lucky if the original spirit and theme of a piece survives the transition from page to film. The particulars of *Newsies* were altered to varying degrees. When Teddy Roosevelt saves the day, we may object because it diminishes the newsies' victory. We may prefer the music of Boots' Place, a precursor-jazz club, over the vaudeville theater owned by a Jenny Lind-style singer. But the basic story, characters, and spirit of what we had written survived.

Caren set up pitch meetings with nine producers' development executives. All passed, until we came to Marianne Sweeny at Finnell/Dante Productions. Marianne listened to our interminable

Playing games in the newsboys' reading room, Boston, MA (Lewis Hine)

pitch and at the end she swore that she would make this happen. We had unleashed a force of nature. She strong-armed her reluctant boss into letting her set up two meetings, with Amblin Entertainment (Steven Spielberg) and Disney. The Disney meeting was scheduled first, by chance. We walked onto a studio lot for the first time as writers, not actors, and did our 45-minute pitch for film executive Donald DeLine. By the next day, we had a verbal deal, which was laughably small but significant to us in 1989.

I was set to do what turned out to be my last film as an actor, *Total Recall*, shooting in Mexico City. A couple of days' work stretched into two weeks, and we still had no word on whether we had actually sold *Newsies* (as in contract signed). I remember watching the protest in Tiananmen Square in our hotel room. This was a milestone event for news coverage, popularizing CNN and 24-hour news. There we were, two Americans in a Japanese hotel in Mexico, riveted by a live feed of events unfolding in China. The world was shrinking and the nature and impact of media were changing. The newsies' 1899 fight for fairness was mirrored by the youth of China as they faced down real tanks 89 years and 11 months later. Although we would of course alter some historical details of *Newsies* for dramatic impact, the importance of getting the newsies' story right hit home—we owed it to them.

New York City circa 1899

EXPLOSION EXTRA NO. 5

The World.

RACING SPORTS

DEVERY'S ESTIMATE OF FIRE HORROR

KILLED AND INJURED PLACED AT 450!

SOME OF THE IDENTIFIED VICTIMS

YELLOW JOURNALISM

"Yellow journalism" was coined in the 1890s to describe sensational and often inaccurate reporting designed to increase the circulation of newspapers. Joseph Pulitzer of *The New York World* and William Randolph Hearst of *The New York Journal* notoriously exaggerated and invented headlines to outsell each other's publications. In February 1898, the U.S.S. *Maine* battleship was sunk in Cuba's Havana Harbor, killing 266 crewmen on board. Although the cause of the explosion was still unclear, these two New York newspapers claimed that the Spanish empire sank the ship. Spain soon declared war on the United States. President William McKinley had wanted to avoid conflict, but quickly followed suit by declaring war on Spain. Beginning in April, battles were fought in the Spanish colonies of Cuba, Puerto Rico, Guam, and the Philippines. Hearst's and Pulitzer's newspapers fuelled the U.S. interest in the Spanish-American War—often described as the first "media war"—and business boomed.

The Tread Mill by C. R. Macauley for the *New York World* c. 1913

CHILD LABOR

In the United States, the idea that kids should go to school to prepare for their future is relatively new. Throughout most of American history, it was normal for children to work long hours at difficult and dangerous jobs. As the number of factories increased during the Industrial Revolution, so did the number of jobs. Factory owners needed more workers and turned to children to help do everything from operating dangerous machinery to mining coal. It was expected that children as young as 10 work 12 or more hours per day for six days a week. According to the U.S. Census of 1880, one in six American children were employed. This number does not account for the number of children under 10 working illegally in sweatshops or on the streets. In 1881, only seven states had education laws requiring kids to attend school, but even in these states, many people found ways to get around the law.

By the turn of the 20th century, when *Newsies* is set, the child workforce hit its peak with almost two million legal and countless undocumented working children. During this period, reformers began to take action and created child labor laws, fought to end the abuse of kids in the workplace, and worked to make sure that all children had the opportunity to better themselves through education. It was not until 1938 that Congress passed the Fair Labor Standards Act, which prohibited the employment of kids younger than 16, and placed limits on the employment of children between 16 and 18 years old.

NEWSIES

Selling newspapers was a lucrative and freeing enterprise for young children at the turn of the 20th century. The newsies of New York City were popularly admired as "little merchants," for unlike children working in factories, the newsboys were free to set their own hours and determine how many papers they would sell each day. However, the newspaper controlled the wholesale price and boys commonly worked up to 14 hours a day to make enough money to survive. It wasn't unusual for a newsboy to exaggerate the headlines or make up sad stories about themselves to sell more papers. They would often fumble and stall while making change in the hopes that the customer would get impatient and let them keep the difference.

If a boy did not have a family to go home to at night, the Newsboys' Lodging House provided them with a place to stay. Each boy paid about 6 cents per night for the accommodations and an additional 4 cents for dinner. If there was a slow news day, the boys might have to choose between the two. The lodging house was located at 49 Park Place in downtown New York City and provided shelter for up to 250 newsboys per night, about 8,000 boys per year. The boys who couldn't afford to stay at the lodging house usually slept in alleys. Newsboys were so commonplace in 19th-century cities that they became symbols of carefree adventures for writers such as Horatio Alger and examples of the ills of child labor for reformers like Lewis Hine and Jacob Riis. Both Hine and Riis photographed newsboys on the streets and in their lodgings to draw public attention to the poor and harsh conditions in which they lived.

FOUNDATIONS OF THE STRIKE

The newsboys' strike depicted in *Newsies* is one of several that have taken place in New York City: 1886, 1890, 1893, 1898, 1899, 1908, 1918, 1922, 1941, and 1948. However, the strike that occurred during the summer of 1899 was the most significant in terms of duration and outcome. The Spanish-American War in 1898 had sparked a boom in the newspaper business. Circulations exploded as customers snatched up papers as fast as they could, eager for news from the front. Newspapers did everything they could to outmatch one another and spent exorbitant amounts of money in eye-catching front pages and eyewitness accounts. To make up some of the money, they raised the wholesale price for the newsboys from 50 to 60 cents per hundred. The newsboys didn't feel the pinch as much because they were enjoying a rise in their profits from the additional demand. But by the summer of 1899, the war had long ended and circulation declined. Almost all of the papers rolled their wholesale price back to 50 cents, except Pulitzer's *World* and Hearst's *Journal*. As the newsboys sold fewer papers each week, the cost difference became harder to manage, and a strike commenced against these two papers beginning July 20, 1899. The publishers did not take the strike seriously until advertisers started making requests to get their bills adjusted. After the successful resolution of the newsboys' strike nearly two weeks after it began, two other children's strikes quickly followed in New York City: the shine boys wanted a wage increase, and messengers were opposed to the 50-cent "tax" they were being charged every week for their uniforms. An irreversible revolution of child laborers had begun.

"Because of the timing of the editions and the hundreds of thousands of customers anxious to get their papers on their way home from work, no newspaper ever had enough newsies. As every circulation manager, city editor, advertising director, and publisher knew, the boys were the last and most vital link in the business chain. Without large numbers out on the streets, crying their wares, advertising their papers, exciting and interesting the public in the latest news and the latest edition, the newspaper business would have been in serious trouble."

—DAVID NASAW

Leading Players

Kid Blink (Louis Ballatt), newsboys' union leader, was blind in one eye and named for his signature eye patch. A ragamuffin who led the New York newsboys in their fight for justice during the summer of 1899, Kid Blink was an inspiration for the character of Jack Kelly. He was often quoted in newspapers covering the strike. Writers sometimes used the phonetic spelling of his speeches in an effort to keep his dialect intact for the entertainment of readers. He and the other newsies allegedly found this style of reporting condescending.

"Friends and fellow workers. This is a time which tries the hearts of men. This is a time when we've got to stick together like glue. We know what we want and we'll get it even if we are blind. I don't agree with you boys about going up and taking papers away from people. What we want is to stick together and not sell *The Journal* and *World*. 10 cents in the dollar is as much to us as it is to Mr. Hearst, the millionaire. Am I right boys? We can do more with 10 cents than he can with 25. I don't believe in hitting the drivers of the news wagons. I don't believe in dumping the carts, same as was done in Madison Street last night. I'll tell you the truth. I was one of the boys that did it, but it ain't right. Just stick together and we'll win."

— KID BLINK, newsboys' rally at New Irving Hall, July 24, 1899, as quoted in *The New York Times* and *The New York Tribune*

Nellie Bly (1864–1922), journalist, was the pen name of Elizabeth Jane Cochrane. In a time when female reporters did not cover much beyond the society pages, Bly made a name for herself as a legitimate journalist. She reported on her record-breaking trip around the world and even faked a mental illness to report on the experience of a patient in a mental institution. Kara Lindsay was inspired by Bly as she developed the character of Katherine Plumber.

William Randolph Hearst (1863–1951), owner and publisher of *The New York Journal*, was born into a wealthy family in San Francisco. After attending Harvard University, Hearst became the manager of a paper his father owned, *The San Francisco Examiner*. At *The Examiner*, he published stories by some of the best writers of the time, including Mark Twain and Jack London. In 1895, he decided to purchase *The New York Morning Journal*, becoming a fierce competitor for Joseph Pulitzer and *The New York World*. Hearst became so successful in the newspaper business that at the peak of his career, he owned over 20 newspapers across the United States. Hearst died at the age of 88 in 1951. Although Hearst is not a character in *Newsies*, his son makes a cameo appearance in a clutch moment.

Lewis Wickes Hine (1874–1940), photographer, was a New York City schoolteacher who felt so strongly about the problem of child labor that he quit his job to take photographs for the National Child Labor Committee. He understood that a picture could be a powerful tool to make the public comprehend the ills brought about by child labor in America.

Mother Jones (Mary Harris Jones, 1837–1930), reformer, visited the Kensington Textile Mills near Philadelphia in 1903 and was horrified when she saw what had happened to the child workers. Most of them were only nine or 10 years old and many had lost fingers or crushed bones by working with dangerous machines. Mother Jones organized the children and took them on a cross-country "Children's Crusade" that led them to the home of President Theodore Roosevelt. Although the president refused to see them, Mother Jones brought the issue of child labor to a much wider audience. In *Newsies*, Katherine's article for *The Newsies Banner* is called "The Children's Crusade" in honor of Mother Jones.

Joseph Pulitzer (1847–1911), owner and publisher of *The New York World*, was born in Hungary in 1847. At the age of 17, after the death of his father, Pulitzer immigrated to the United States to enlist in the Union Army. At the end of the Civil War, he traveled from New York City to St. Louis to find a job. After three years of working as a fireman, dockworker, waiter, and gravedigger, Pulitzer was offered a job writing for the German newspaper, *The Westliche Post.* Despite his poor eyesight, he was so successful that he was named managing editor and eventually purchased *The St. Louis Dispatch*, one of the major newspapers in the city. Pulitzer purchased *The New York World* in 1883 and turned the failing paper into one of the most widely read publications in the city. The articles that *The World* published about the sinking of the U.S.S. *Maine* battleship were a large contributor to the start of the Spanish-American War. Although the historical Pulitzer was not an active player in the newsboys' strike, his character in *Newsies* is an antagonist who represents the excesses of capitalism. Pulitzer married American Kate Davis in 1878, and by the time of the strike, he had become the rather distant father of seven children: Ralph (20), Lucille (18), Katherine (17), Joseph, Jr. (14), Edith (13), Constance (10), and Herbert (3). Ralph took over *The World* upon his father's death in 1911 at the age of 64. Pulitzer left enough money to Columbia University to start a journalism school. The Pulitzer Prize, an award for excellence in journalism, literature, and music, was named in his honor.

Jacob Riis (1849-1914), photojournalist, was born in Denmark in 1849 and immigrated to the United States in 1870. He began work as a police reporter for *The New York Tribune* in 1877 and soon after was employed as a photojournalist for *The New York Evening Sun.* Sometimes referred to as one of the fathers of photography, Riis published a photo-account of poverty in the city, *How the Other Half Lives*, in 1890. His work later caught the eye of President Theodore Roosevelt, and the two became lifelong friends. Riis spent much of his professional life documenting impoverished children and laborers in the nation's urban centers. In *Newsies*, Jack's illustrations of the horrors of The Refuge lead to its closure and the arrest of its warden, Snyder.

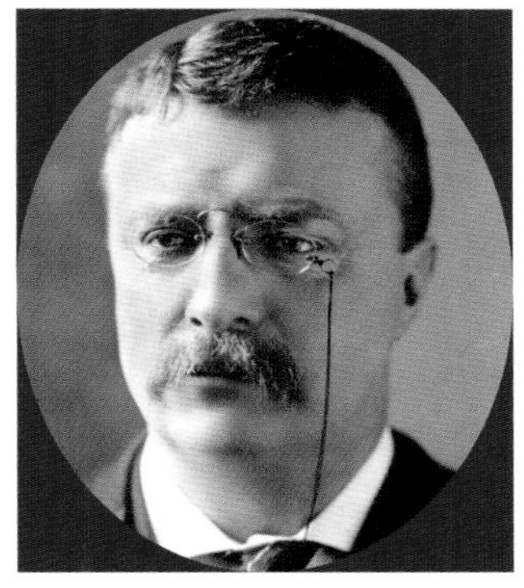

Theodore Roosevelt (1858–1919), 33rd governor of New York, previously served as a New York State Assembly member, United States Civil Service commissioner, president of the New York Board of Police Commissioners, and assistant secretary of the Navy. As the leader of the "Rough Riders" during the Spanish-American War in 1898, Roosevelt became a national hero and was elected governor of New York later that year. As governor, he improved labor laws, outlawed racial segregation in public schools, and advanced park and forestry programs. Although Roosevelt and Pulitzer were often on opposite political sides, their interaction over the strike in Newsies is fictional. In 1900, Roosevelt became vice president under William McKinley and assumed the presidency after McKinley's assassination in 1901. Roosevelt was reelected as the Republican nominee three years later.

Robert Van Wyck (1849–1918), 91st mayor of New York, began his public career as a judge and later rose to chief justice of the City Court of New York, working closely with Tammany Hall, the city's powerful Democratic Party political machine. In 1898, he became mayor of New York, and the first to preside over the newly incorporated five boroughs. Mayor Van Wyck also awarded the city's first subway contract, valued at $35 million. In 1900, he was implicated in an Ice Trust scandal by owning a large sum of shares in the American Ice Company before it planned to double the price of ice from 30 to 60 cents per 100 pounds. The American Ice Company was the sole ice provider for the city, and therefore an illegal monopoly. An investigation was conducted by Governor Roosevelt. Although the mayor was found to be not guilty, the scandal cost him the election in 1901. Van Wyck continued to work as a lawyer and in 1906 moved to Paris, where he lived until his death in 1918.

Aida Overton Walker (1880–1914), performer, was one of the premiere African American artists at the turn of the 20th century, known for her original dance routines and refusal to conform to the stereotype of traditional black female performers. Overton had a successful career as a star of the Bowery and beyond. She married fellow performer George Walker in 1898, and the pair became one of the most revered African American couples on the stage. Before her death in 1914, Walker worked hard to aid young black women striving to make a name for themselves. She organized benefits in honor of the Industrial Home for Colored Working Girls and played an active role in the development of young black women as stage performers. Walker served as inspiration when the character of Medda Larkin was reconceived between the Paper Mill and Broadway productions.

Historical Newsies of 1899

Although thousands of newsboys participated in the strike, these names were listed in newspaper articles covering the events:

David Simons*
Jack Harney**
Kid Blink
Racetrack Higgins
Crutch Morris
Henry Butler
Barney Peanuts
Morris Cohen
Blind Diamond
Bob Indian
Crazy Arborn
Edward Fitzgerald
Jim Gaiety
Little Mike
Nick Myers
Scabutch
Young Monix
Annie Kelly***

** President of the Newsboys' Union*
*** Offered $600 to call off strike and charged with extortion and blackmail*
**** Ran a newspaper stand, was a huge supporter of the boys in their strike, and spoke during the rally at New Irving Hall*

Time Line

May 24, 1883—The New York and Brooklyn Bridge is completed, uniting two of the world's largest cities.

December 10, 1890—At the Manhattan end of the Brooklyn Bridge, Joseph Pulitzer's 349-foot World Building is completed, becoming the tallest building on Earth and casting a huge shadow over City Hall Park.

May 4, 1897—The charter of "Greater New York" becomes law, under which the city of New York incorporates Brooklyn, Queens, the Bronx, and Richmond (later Staten Island) with Manhattan under a new government that would take effect the following year.

February 15, 1898—The U.S.S. *Maine* is sunk by a mysterious explosion in Havana Harbor, Cuba.

April 25, 1898—The Spanish-American War begins.

August 12, 1898—The Spanish-American War ends.

July 19, 1899—Dissent among the newsies due to a price hike builds to a head and word spreads of a strike commencing the following day.

July 20, 1899—The newsboys refuse to sell *The World* and *The Journal.* Jersey City newsboys join with their New York brethren in a strike against the papers.

July 22, 1899—Newsie leader Kid Blink meets Hearst outside of his office.

July 24, 1899—*The World* and *The Journal* do not give in to the newsies' demands. The publishers hire men to sell their papers, paying them as much as $2 per day.

July 24, 1899—A mass meeting of newsboys is held at New Irving Hall. 2,000 boys fit inside the theater and another 3,000 observe from the street.

July 25, 1899—Pulitzer and Hearst agree to lower the newsboys' price from 60 cents to 55 cents per hundred. The newsboys decline the offer, deciding to hold out.

Michael McNeils, age eight, Philadelphia, PA (Lewis Hine)

July 27, 1899—Kid Blink leaves the newsboys' union. Rumors spread that he accepted a bribe from the publishers.

August 1, 1899—The publishers agree to buy back unsold papers from the newsies. Satisfied with this historic compromise, the newsboys call off the strike.

August 2, 1899—The newsies of New York return to work, carrying the banner.

"The newsies had to decide for themselves how many papers to purchase each afternoon. That was no easy task. Every paper purchased from the circulation manager had to be unloaded before the next edition came out. If the children bought too many papers, they would have to swallow the loss on the unsold copies or stay out all night to sell them—and that became progressively more difficult as it got later and the street traffic thinned. If, on the other hand, they bought too few, they stood in danger of losing customers."

— DAVID NASAW

Torey Sorel, Memphis, TN

Meghan Brown, Malden, MA

Brenna Corporal, Massa

“I’ve always been interested in labor history and women’s history, and I’m so happy more people are learning about it through these characters. When I came to see the show, I got a chance to visit the Tenement Museum, which reminded me how important it is that these stories be told.”

— Laura McVey, Ancaster, Canada

Laura McVey, Ancaster, Canada

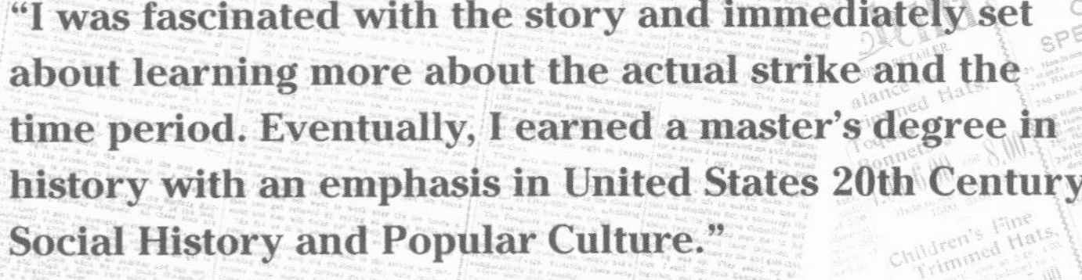

“I was fascinated with the story and immediately set about learning more about the actual strike and the time period. Eventually, I earned a master’s degree in history with an emphasis in United States 20th Century Social History and Popular Culture.”

— Mercedes Anderson, Long Beach, CA

Daniela Diaz Jarquin, Tarrytown, NY

“*Newsies* teaches a valuable lesson of determination. No matter how much the world will cut you down, as long as you have the courage—and loved ones by your side—nothing will stop you from becoming what you were born to be.”

— Kara Walton,
Birmingham, AL

Amy Manske, New London, WI

Jeanette Logan, Mount Gilead, OH

Allison Wagner, Holbrook, NY

Ivan Joshua, Indonesia

"*Newsies* takes a small historical event and invigorates a new generation with the passion and determination to make a difference. I'm a journalism student, and there is nothing as fantastic as watching one young girl defy society and start a revolutionary movement because she knows what is right. I'm at a crossroads in my life, and this show gave me the determination to take the harder path, because it's the one that's right for me. *Newsies* is not just a musical; it's a movement."

— Annamarie Carlson, Canal Winchester, OH

Kara Hynes, Chicago, IL

"The whole purpose of *Newsies* is standing up for what you believe in. As a deaf person, I've not always gotten what I needed to be successful. But having to stand up for myself, I've gotten it. If you have a dream, go for it. Nothing can stop you from achieving it except yourself."

— Justin Drezner, Princeton, NJ

Gabriella Trentacoste, New Orleans, LA

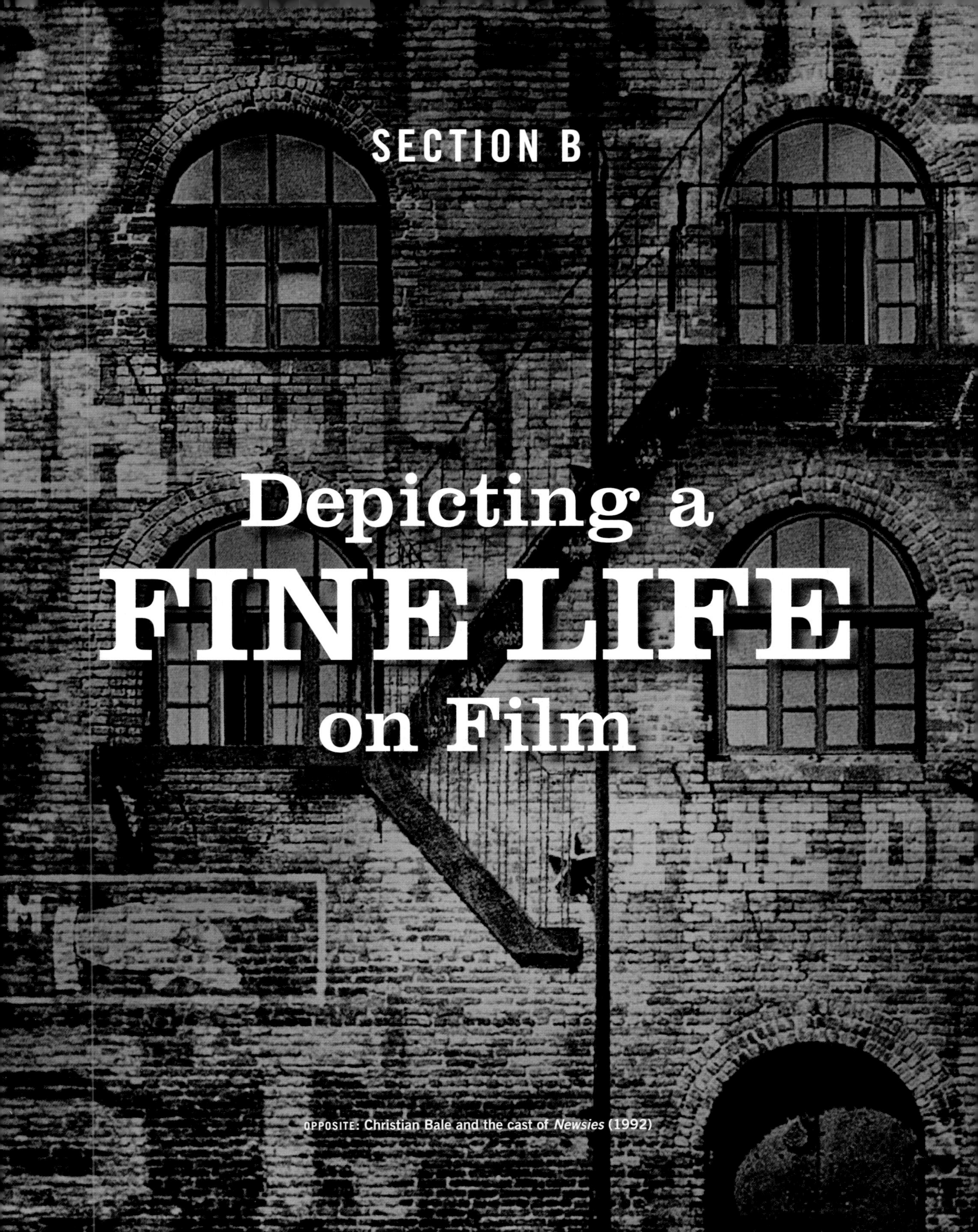

SECTION B

Depicting a FINE LIFE on Film

OPPOSITE: Christian Bale and the cast of *Newsies* (1992)

Dreaming Big and Letting Go

Noni White
co-screenwriter, *Newsies* (1992)

When Bob Tzudiker (my husband and partner) first asked me what I thought of working on a story about the newsboys' strike of 1899, I said, "That's the quintessential David-and-Goliath story." It felt big and important and incredibly rich, a story that needed to be told. That was in the late 1980s, and ever since I have been envisioning *Newsies* on Broadway—against all odds. Bob is a much more linear thinker than I am; the only time my thoughts go in a straight line is when I'm envisioning something. My father died tragically when I was very young. I had what they now call "learning disabilities" in a time when no one knew what that meant. But I always projected in my mind's eye that all would be well. Day-dreaming, which some people think is a waste of time, is a form of envisioning. It got me through school, and it's how I've made my living. So the little girl who stuttered, couldn't sit still, and didn't read her first book until she was 20 has grown to become a successful actress and writer.

Of course, a dream doesn't always come true, and even when it does, the details may not match up. A lot of the final film of *Newsies* didn't ultimately match our script, and there are parts of the stage show that don't fit our original vision of the piece. But in these vast collaborations, many people have to express their vision, and being among the first doesn't mean I'm right. Some subtleties did not survive, but core values came through. I swear this thing has a beating heart that will not stop.

Jack was a combination of many real-life newsies, including Kid Blink and a newsie named Morris. In our original scripts, Jack longed to go to Santa Fe because he was hoping to reunite with his little brother, who had been sent west on an orphan train. There was also an accident in Jack's past, and he felt responsible for the death of a young newsie whom he had been training to be his partner. I've always loved Jack's character—his toughness, his sweetness, his bravado—and I've so enjoyed seeing him come to life again.

David and Les are very much who they were in our many early drafts. They lived with their parents and sister, Sarah, who ended up becoming the love interest in our later drafts. We had read somewhere during our research that one out of 10 newsies were girls, so we were sad not to see one on film or stage. For the first five drafts of our script, a girl named Charlie (who wore her long hair tucked under her newsie cap) was head over heels in love with Jack. He thought of Charlie as one of the guys, but in the end it was Charlie who accompanied Jack on the train to Santa Fe. I think the reason Charlie morphed into Sarah in the film was because Charlie lived in a brothel with her Aunt Louise. Aunt Louise didn't want Charlie going into "the life"; she wanted a better future for her niece. When we sold our pitch to Disney, I said to Bob, "The brothel's going to go."

Boots was based on a real newsie who went from shining shoes to selling papers. We created his parents and uncle, who owned the honky-tonk, "Boots' Place," where the kids hung out and would go to celebrate. These relatives also helped the newsies fight off the thugs who were sent to beat their heads in. In the film, Boots' Place became the soda fountain where they sing "King of New York," my favorite number.

Kenny Ortega was a first-time director getting input from many different sources, yet he was so welcoming to us. We were juggling several projects at the time, but whenever we showed up, we were always invited on the set. Kenny let us watch dailies and he created an atmosphere of joy and camaraderie that was infectious. He treated everyone with respect. I remember being there the day we had over 1,000 extras for the children's march at the end. We were shooting in the San Fernando Valley and the temperature was well over 100 degrees. Kenny insisted that everyone break for water, to the dismay of many production people. That may sound like a small thing, but it's not, and it speaks to the heart of the film and everyone having a fair shake.

Of course, you want something that means so much to you to be a huge success, so it was incredibly disappointing to see the movie flop. Letting go of high hopes is hard. However, my dreaming has certainly been helped by the fans. When Bob and I are asked to speak at colleges, people tell us that we wrote their favorite movie. The people *Newsies* reached, it touched deeply.

OPPOSITE: Original storyboards for *Newsies* (1992). **RIGHT:** Arvie Lowe Jr., Aaron Lohr, Trey Parker, Max Casella, Luke Edwards, and David Moscow in *Newsies*

The Rapid Evolution of History into Musical

Bob Tzudiker

I do not recall exactly when we learned the *Newsies* movie deal would close. But after we received our first check, I do remember Noni saying she wanted to buy a CD. "But we don't own a CD player," I said. "No!" she said, "a CD, at a bank!" (Noni is big on saving money—and spending it.) A certificate of deposit is what she meant, although both types of CDs are now nearly obsolete.

There's a moment after you sell a project when, no matter how experienced you are, your stomach drops and you realize you have to deliver on the promise of the story you pitched. This would be our second screenplay and our first job. But *Newsies* flew through the process routinely referred to as "development hell." Donald DeLine and Marianne Sweeny guided us to the fastest green light those executives had ever seen. Donald helped us navigate studio notes we disagreed with and title changes we disliked (it was called *Extra!* for a little while). He would subtly signal which battles were worth fighting and which notes, if executed, would snap back to what we liked in a subsequent draft.

Donald did not want *Newsies* to be a musical. He knew it was well suited to the genre, but he believed no one knew how to pull it off. However, Jeffrey Katzenberg, head of the Disney studio at the time, was fresh from the success of *The Little Mermaid*, and he thought the live-action musical was ready for a comeback. So we designed a hybrid in which the situations would, within the natural screen world, lend themselves to music. This was a step removed from a "break into song" musical, in which the screen reality shifts and time expands to allow characters to sing. Our final draft was this hybrid musical, and thus began a brief collaboration with the new key elements of the film: composer Alan Menken, lyricist Jack Feldman, and director Kenny Ortega.

We knew we were extremely vulnerable to being replaced by other writers. This came to pass soon after we delivered our fifth draft. We were hardly surprised, but we were heartbroken. The studio had reorganized into Touchstone and Disney studios, and we lost Donald to Touchstone. Marianne got the ax, and we soon followed. The rush of transition to full-out musical fell to David Fallon and then Tom Rickman, who had to make room in our script for over 20 minutes of song. This musical transition was so fast that potential cast and crew were given our last draft, and some had no idea it was a full-out musical until they began work. At an early camera test, Christian Bale was told

4/22/91 TAN

14 CONTINUED: 9.

14

MOTHER
PATRICK, DARLING...

RACETRACK
JUST GIMME HALF A CUP

KID BLINK
SOMETHING TO WAKE ME UP

SINCE YOU LEFT ME

MUSH
I GOTTA FIND AN ANGLE

I AM UNDONE

CRUTCHY
I GOTTA SELL MORE PAPES

MOTHER
LOVES YOU

ALL
PAPERS IS ALL I GOT
WISH I COULD CATCH A BREEZE
SURE HOPE THE HEADLINE'S HOT
ALL I CAN CATCH IS FLEAS
GOD HELP ME IF IT'S NOT
SOMEBODY HELP ME PL --

GOD
SAVE
MY SON

15 EXT. NEWSIE SQUARE - SAME TIME 15

PULL BACK to reveal entire square as Jack and the gang leave the wagon, cross the square and head for the gates of The World Building, keeping their eyes on the huge blackboards over the street.

ALL
IF I HATE THE HEADLINE
I'LL MAKE UP A HEADLINE
AND I'LL SAY ANYTHING I HAFTA
'CAUSE AT TWO FOR A PENNY
IF I TAKE TOO MANY
WEASEL JUST MAKES ME EAT 'EM
AFTA

Newsies of all ages and sizes appear from every conceivable space and line up outside the gates, waiting for them to open, anxiously praying for a good headline to be chalked on the boards overhead...

16 EXT. NEWSPAPER ROW - SAME TIME 16

Two men climb ladders to the blackboards above the street and start to write out headlines in chalk: "TROLLEY STRIKE DRAGS ON FOR THIRD WEEK."

17 EXT. ALLEY/OFF NEWSIE SQUARE - SAME TIME 17

A GROUP of NEWSIES follow through an alley that leads them to the square, where they see the men chalking up headlines.

(CONTINUED)

Pages from the final shooting script

he'd be singing and dancing across a rooftop. He was mortified: "I don't sing or dance!" He had to make a quick (and courageous) decision whether to continue with the film.

Unbeknownst to us, our first draft of *Newsies* had been read by Disney Feature Animation. As soon as we were available, they asked us to work on a project with director Rob Minkoff (*The Lion King*, *Stuart Little*), Kelly Asbury (*Shrek II*, *Spirit*) and Broadway legend Jerry Herman (*Mame*, *Hello, Dolly!*, *La Cage aux Folles*). That project didn't fly, but it began a wonderful career for us in Feature Animation, working with the executives who later founded Disney Theatrical (Peter Schneider and Thomas Schumacher). While we were working on that first project, we sold our romantic comedy, and the sale was on the front page of *Variety*. We came into our backlot trailer office to find it festooned with tiny dollar bills and a caricature by Kelly of me pushing Noni in a wheelbarrow full of money. It still hangs above the doorway to our office as (we hope) a charm.

Newsies was widely considered a failure in its initial release. But it was rescued from oblivion by changes in media and technology. After its dismal feature debut, it was released on VHS. Then, we are told, the Disney Channel began without enough programming to fill the hours, so the programming chief pulled *Newsies* into his lineup, playing it again and again, exposing millions of young people to the film. That audience drove VHS sales, and later clamored for a DVD when that technology became available. Without the launch of cable channels and home viewing, *Newsies* probably would have disappeared. We were oblivious to all of this. We would be surprised now and then to hear from some excited young person that we had written his or her favorite film. We'd figure it was *Tarzan*, but invariably it would be *Newsies*.

Memo

Re: EXTRA!

Dear Donald,

If the FAX gods are with us, you are holding our list of potential songs. We are very excited at the prospect of these characters singing and dancing. This will be a great musical.

—FROM NONI WHITE AND BOB TZUDIKER
TO DONALD DELINE OF DISNEY STUDIOS
JUNE 15, 1990

To Break into Song—Or Not to Break into Song

Chris Montan
executive music producer

I probably started working on *Newsies* in 1990, because developing all of the songs was a fairly long process. At that point, we had finished the music for *Beauty and the Beast*, so Alan Menken and I were getting pretty experienced at working together. *Beauty* hadn't come out yet, but we were already starting to work on *Newsies*. Howard Ashman was unfortunately pretty sick at this point and was not going to be able to write, so Alan started working with Jack Feldman, a lyricist he had met through the BMI Workshop in the 1970s and always wanted to work with.

Jeffrey Katzenberg wanted to see if we could apply a lot of the things we had learned on *The Little Mermaid* and *Beauty and the Beast* to a live-action project. Bob and Noni's original *Newsies* screenplay was a historic live-action script without a musical intent. They really loved the turn-of-the-century New York period—Pulitzer and the labor force and what was happening to children at that time—with a more serious bent than what the movie ultimately became. They wanted to get it right. Still, Katzenberg felt that *Newsies* might be a good candidate for musical conversion.

But as far as the studio was concerned, we were still pretty under the radar, and the movie didn't cost that much for its time. No one was doing live-action musicals, other than things like *Flashdance*, which were really more montage movies. Nobody was "breaking into song" on the big screen that I can remember. There were a couple of TV

attempts in 1990: *Cop Rock* and *Hull High*. Neither show was successful, and actually *Cop Rock* didn't do well at all. It was trying to be serious and then somebody would all of a sudden break into song. *Hull High* was much lighter and surrounded by cheerleaders and characters that you were used to from those '50s movies. It was on NBC and directed by Kenny Ortega, and I think that's where Jeffrey got the idea that maybe Kenny, who had also done a lot of major choreography, would be suitable to direct *Newsies*.

"Carrying the Banner" was one of the early songs written, as was "Seize the Day." The score was feeling really strong. We recorded the soundtrack down at Ocean Way on Sunset with a very young Christian Bale and a number of other young actors, which was really fun. Like any musical, when you are in development, it is hard to predict where the show is going and where the book will go, but we already knew that we had some really, really strong songs. And we were there for a while. I mean, it was a big score to record. Danny Troob was a one-man wrecking crew on that one. He did almost everything: arranger, orchestrator, conductor, vocal coach. He had a lot of young singing actors and then some actors, especially principals, who weren't necessarily singers, so they needed a lot of help.

As is normal for movie musicals, we got all the songs recorded before production started. "Carrying the Banner" is quite an elaborate number, and producer Mike Finnell showed me a very early rough cut, which felt like a production by a team of people who didn't have a great deal of experience doing it. There were rough spots where music would be cut in places that you wouldn't normally cut it. There were a lot of talented people and some who had studied musicals—certainly Kenny and Alan knew musicals. But there wasn't the kind of support that Feature Animation was able to give *Beauty and the Beast* and *Aladdin*, largely because Howard Ashman had trained us all in that medium. We learned on the job. And with Peter Schneider and Tom Schumacher, there was a lot of theater background in Feature Animation. But most of the senior executives at the studio had never made a live-action musical, so it was natural that there was a big learning curve.

Anytime you are working on a film and you are seeing that rough cuts and/or previews are not playing well, you shift your strategy. We must have had a pretty tough preview at one point, because I remember that Jeffrey came in to do a great deal of cutting. J.A.C. Redford had already scored the film, so when they made 200 little trims here and there, it really knocked our timings off. Jeffrey wasn't wrong to try to tighten the film, but a lot of it was rough on the final musical score.

We've learned over the years that successful musicals are really about a consistency and confidence of tone. As you go back and watch *Newsies* now, you see it's got a lot of different elements. Sometimes it feels like a live-action movie. Sometimes it feels shot on a studio lot. A lot of the scenes with Robert Duvall as Pulitzer in the office feel almost like shot plays. If you then look at Rob Marshall's film of *Chicago*, that movie is so confident from beginning to end. It was shot as a fantasy because there are a lot of stylized moments in the storytelling, like "Cell Block Tango" and "Mr. Cellophane." *Newsies* was trying to walk that really uncomfortable line between realism and musical comedy. I think that was its undoing—it just wasn't unified that way. And I think the studio executives knew it. I mean, the testing numbers were really bad.

I remember that within a year of opening, I wished I had gone back in and said, "I think we should make this a holiday Christmas special and show it on television instead." The budget wasn't that big, but we were going to lose the money anyway. If we could start to make it an annual Christmas thing, we might be able to collect license fees and create a different home-video event for the movie. But that is a lot of hindsight. I just had a feeling that no one was going to accept the "break into song" part. I'd already seen it happen with *Hull High* and *Cop Rock*, and nobody could show me that people really wanted to watch actors break into song in 1992, at least in a live-action film on the big screen.

Animation was a different story, as were live-action movies on the small screen. A few years later, in the late 1990s, after *Newsies* had picked up steam on the Disney Channel and home video, I produced television movies of both *Cinderella* and *Annie* with Craig Zadan and Neil Meron. And we had a market survey that showed that people were fine with actors breaking into song if they were in their homes. We used to have viewing parties for my son and his friends, who were 14 or 15 and probably would never have gone to the movie theater to see *Newsies* or *Annie* but loved watching them on TV at home. I came into the room one time and they were doing a kick line, like six of them. I think there was a certain stigma attached to musicals and so, if you were a teenager, it wasn't cool to go to the movie theater to see one. But it was fine to watch it at home!

The One-Man Wrecking Crew

Danny Troob
orchestrator and film music arranger and conductor

I am one of the few who worked on *Newsies*, the movie, and also *Newsies*, the stage show. When I started work on the movie, in 1991, I was in my early 40s. *Newsies* was my second project at Disney (after *Beauty and the Beast*) and the first where I spent a long period of time in California. My job had a wide range of responsibilities: writing the orchestrations, vocal arrangements, and dance music, and conducting the song sessions. I worked with Kenny Ortega every day in the studio. I taught the newsies their vocals. I worked on the set. I worked in the recording studios. I met lots of people and made lots of new friends. We had as many musicians, and as much time, as we needed for each track. It was enormous fun, and who knew what it could lead to?

Then the movie came out. We were a disaster at the box office. David Letterman told *Newsies* jokes in his monologue. Or was it Jay Leno? I can't remember. But I do remember that at other projects at Disney, people became very aloof, very quickly, after our inglorious opening. They would just get busy with the water fountain or duck into someone's office when I walked down the corridor. For it is always better to be associated with hits than with flops. After *Beauty and the Beast*, I was to have my share of more hits later on with *Aladdin* and many other projects. But I forgot about *Newsies* and didn't listen to the CD for almost 20 years.

Hollywood Dreams

Max Casella

Racetrack Higgins

By 1991, I had been performing on stage and television for a decade, but I had never been in a feature film. I dove into my first movie project, Disney's live-action musical film *Newsies*, with great enthusiasm. When I got the role, I called up writers Bob Tzudiker and Noni White to ask if I could have access to their research materials on the 1899 newsboys strike. They kindly directed me to the Los Angeles Public Library, where I practically moved in, looking at microfilms of old newspaper articles of the period (no Google yet!).

I studied Jacob Riis's phenomenal photo book, *How the Other Half Lives*. The real history of the newsboys fascinated me. The reality of these kids' lives was much, much darker than what we ultimately represented in the film. Most of them slept in the streets, and during the strike many were killed. To my mind, they were like little men: they didn't go to school, they worked for a living, and they dressed like adults. My character, Racetrack, wore a vest and pocket watch. I fancied him a bit of an Artful Dodger. I still have *How the Other Half Lives* here on my shelf . . . L.A. Public Library—DUE April 19, 1991. Oops.

Anyway, filming at the Universal backlot in the Valley started in April. There was such excitement on set with everyone really believing that the movie was going to be a huge hit. The cast bonded so well that we even spent our downtime shooting a homemade horror movie: *Blood Drips Heavily on Newsie Square*. Most of the guys were from Southern California, but I grew up in Cambridge, Massachusetts, with a mom from Long Island and a dad from the Bronx. Although my accent was a hodgepodge of Boston and Bronx, I guess I sounded the most like a newsie, so the rest of the cast came to me for advice on capturing the right dialect—all of which added up to really enthusiastic but totally fake New York accents!

Max Casella as Racetrack Higgins

"King of New York"

It was a real shock to witness the movie bomb when it premiered the next spring. A crushing disappointment, actually. For the next several years, it seemed like Disney tried to forget that *Newsies* even existed, as if it were an embarrassment you didn't bring up in conversation. Even by

1997, when I was cast as Timon in the stage production of *The Lion King*, Disney folks still didn't really talk about it.

But around the same time, I caught wind that a *Newsies* cult following had developed. Kids discovered the movie on the Disney Channel and VHS, and *Newsies* found other fans on the Internet, which gave people a new, virtual space to congregate. A friend told me to do an online search for "Newsies" and I found lists upon lists of chat rooms and fan sites. Kids were so devoted to the movie that they were even doing their own stage adaptations at their schools and camps. It blew my mind!

Fast-forward 15 years and I'm sitting at the Broadway opening of *Newsies* next to the film's director, Kenny Ortega. The whole experience was surreal. It brought back a very special time in my life—the summer of 1991 where I was splitting my time between a hit TV series and filming *Newsies*, sharing my apartment with my first live-in girlfriend, and driving my old Cadillac "Francis" to and from the set. All those memories came flooding back as I watched a new generation of performers onstage. It was a very moving and personal event.

Newsies Obsession Develops

Aaron Albano

Finch

My first experience with *Newsies* was when I saw it in the movie theater. I'm one of the few members of our cast who is old enough to have actually seen it in the theater. It was the first time I'd seen a live-action musical with guys dancing. At that time I hadn't really started training yet, but I saw the movie and became obsessed with it, just like others of my generation did. A lot of people claim *Newsies* as their own, but musicals have only come back into mainstream recently. Kids born in the 1980s grew up with musicals that were animated. I think that's one of the main reasons that *Newsies* was a flop, because the live-action musical was a dead breed. People don't sing and dance; mermaids, beasts, and lions sing and dance. Now with *Chicago*, *Glee*, and *Smash*, it's returned to being cool. When you're nine to 12 years old, watching something new matters. My generation had *Newsies*, whereas the 1990s kids had *High School Musical*. When the screen is grainy, you assume it was made for your parents' generation. *Mary Poppins* is a great movie, but it was made in the 1960s and you can tell. It's the same way a kid now can tell *Newsies* was made in 1992. As much as *Newsies* was a big part of my childhood, I wouldn't say I recognized the cult following. At the time, I didn't know what a cult following was. But I was a part of it. (*Rent*-heads don't realize they're crazy people who like *Rent* because they're them.) I was one of the very first Fansies. Did I know what Fansies were? Of course not. But did I love this movie? Of course. And I had a worn-out VHS tape. I think it's still at my childhood home in San Jose. I taped it off the Disney Channel at some point. I now have the Blu-Ray. I had the DVD, but I gave it to the kids' dressing room at the Nederlander Theatre. I don't need it anymore.

Emily Powell

assistant company manager

I honestly don't remember the first time I saw *Newsies*. And I don't remember when it became my favorite movie. What I do remember clearly is renting *Newsies* when my family traveled to a beach house in Ventura, California. It was the mid-'90s, and whether we spent the weekend there with cousins, friends, or no one beyond our immediate family, amid board games and time on the beach, I would head to the local video store to check out *Newsies*. On one such trip, I asked the sales clerk at the store if I could purchase the video and take it home. He responded with the store's

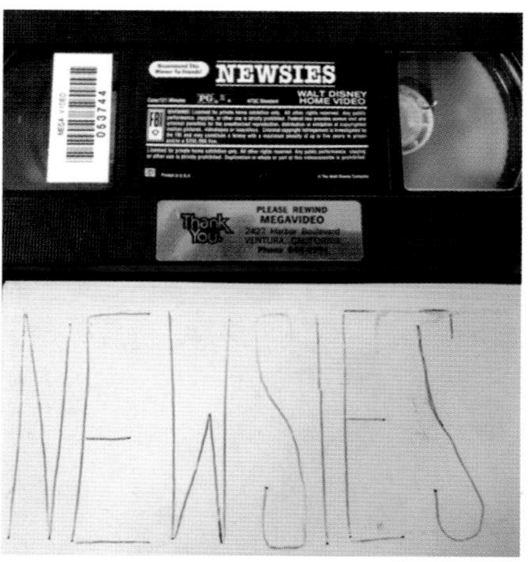

Emily Powell's prized possession

policy: no sales, only rentals. So I asked again, "How much would it take to buy the VHS?" Again, the answer came: "We don't sell movies; we rent them." I made one final plea, at which point the kid behind the counter decided to look into his computer to see when *Newsies* was last rented. It had been two years. The last person to rent it? Yours truly. He finally sold it to me for $10.

Colleen McCormack

creative coordinator, DTG

My *Newsies* journey began when I was about eight years old and saw the movie on the Disney Channel. My brother and I loved the story and the music so much that we scoured video store after video store and finally found one that had it in stock, just so we could watch it again. After probably the 100th viewing, our VHS tape gave out and jammed our VCR. But by that time we had memorized the entire thing and were giving command performances for our parents in the living room. I got the *Newsies* vocal selections book for my birthday and spent the next several weeks glued to the piano learning every note. It wasn't until I went to college that I realized other people my age had the same devotion to this "little-known" movie. We would regularly hold screenings (when we could find someone who still had a VCR) and drag in any of our uninitiated friends.

Christian Bale as Jack Kelly

Marty Belafsky as Crutchy

Christopher Gattelli

stage choreographer

There was kind of a groundswell when I was a teen that there was this movie happening in L.A. with male dancers my age. And it was exciting to hear about. I remember sitting in the movie theater and being blown away seeing that many guys my age dancing like that. And at the time—before YouTube and all the social media and all these links where you have access to everything—I just remember sitting there and being so inspired. I saw that it was possible to be a guy and be able to dance like that. There were so many out there and how great they all were . . . it was pretty life-changing. I remember feeling such a high after seeing it.

Lou Castro

associate choreographer

I started dancing at the age of five. When I was eight, I met this amazing teacher from The Dance Theatre of Harlem who made dancing so much fun that I sometimes forgot I was dancing. Gary's dance studio felt like a playground. He passed away when I was 10, and because of that I ended up quitting dance altogether. I was like, "Okay, I'm going to be a cop." Fast-forward two years and *Newsies* came out. As I watched it, I had flashbacks of how much fun dancing used to be. How can you not want to dance after seeing that movie? Around that same time, my friend's mom called and said they had found a new dance studio and thought I should go and try it out. The decision for me to dance again became so easy after watching *Newsies*. I started dancing six days a week, eight hours a day. And even

David Moscow as David

THE MUSICAL
NEWSIES
A Thousand Voices.
A Single Dream.
WALT DISNEY PICTURES "NEWSIES" MICHAEL FINNELL
CHRISTIAN BALE BILL PULLMAN ROBERT DUVALL
ALAN MENKEN JACK FELDMAN J.A.C. REDFORD PEGGY HOLMES
WILLIAM SANDELL ANDREW LASZLO, A.S.C. BOB TZUDIKER NONI WHITE MICHAEL FINNELL KENNY ORTEGA
PG PARENTAL GUIDANCE SUGGESTED
SOME MATERIAL MAY NOT BE SUITABLE FOR CHILDREN
DOLBY STEREO

"The premise for *Newsies*, an elaborate Disney live-action musical about the New York newsboys' strike of 1899, never sounded all that promising in the first place. . . . Many of the musical numbers are staged so strangely that the characters, when they begin singing, appear to have taken leave of their senses."

—JANET MASLIN, *The New York Times*, April 8, 1992

though Gary wasn't around anymore, dancing in a studio still felt like playing on a playground. Thanks Gary!

Eduardo Castro

production manager/company manager

I do recall seeing *Newsies* when it came out and liking it a lot. Back then I started to have that love for musicals. What I remember the most out of the film was "Once and For All"—that beat going fast and all the kids passing out papers always stuck with me. I also remember that iconic poster outside the movie theater.

"The real problem . . . is that the picture just seems grossly out of touch with its times; it's a retrograde item, and fatiguingly square. . . . A new twist, a rethinking, a fresh wrinkle is what's needed."

—HAL HINSON, *The Washington Post*, April 10, 1992

But then *Newsies* kind of went away from my life. I didn't really have that VCR tape that I ran 20,000 times. But I did have the soundtrack—on cassette. I used to ask my dad to put it in the car and play it on the way to school. I was in love with the music. Like, in love. There was something very special and very youthful, something that I really connected with, whether it was the lyrics or the rhythm or just the idea of being able to be with a bunch of friends and just kind of burst out into song and dance. That was such a foreign thing to me because I had just moved from Mexico, leaving behind the friends and daily activities that I knew so well. Now being in a whole different country with different traditions and a different language, there was something about the *Newsies* music that I just liked, that just kind of kept me going. God, that is so cheesy, but it is so true, now that I think about it. *Newsies* is one of those things you connect with so deeply—it just gets in your fibers. There is a little bit of longing, of dreaming, and at the same time a call to action . . . that you can't just stop and wait for things to happen, you have to take control. That music makes you want to do that.

Justin Huff

casting director

Growing up in northern Indiana, I had a dream of singing and dancing onstage. However, musicals were not something I ever thought one could ever pursue as a career, especially boys. It was my love of *Newsies* that helped me realize I could dream bigger. As a kid, my family would make a weekly trip to the local video store. It was there that I first came across a little-known Disney film: *Newsies*. I remember being intrigued by the film's tagline on the video's cover: "They found the courage to challenge the powerful." The day I took that video to the checkout counter, my life was changed. I will never forget watching the film for the first time. As a boy who loved performing, the movie blew my mind! It challenged my belief that musicals weren't cool. Finally, there was something that allowed me to believe that cool guys do musicals. Christian Bale's rough-and-tumble Jack Kelly leading the powerful newsboys as they danced through the streets of Manhattan did more than fight the evil Pulitzer. He gave permission for boys like me to follow their dreams of performing. In the years that followed, I remember wondering if *Newsies* would ever be a stage musical. I hoped that if it ever did, I would have a chance to be a part of it.

Michael Fatica

Swing, dance captain

Halloween is the most anticipated day of the year for kids all around the country. This is the one day where we have free reign to dress up as whoever we want to be, whether realistic or fantastical (some past Fatica favorites include two years as the red Power Ranger and one painstaking night as the Terminator). As actors, we have the privilege of getting to explore someone else's life every day, and I can't think of a better life to be a part of than that of a newsie. Back in the seventh grade, I was commissioned to be a newsboy in a play, which was thrilling on two very important levels: *Newsies* was one of my favorite movies, and newsboy caps were already becoming retro and awesome, so I didn't have to sacrifice any style for the show. Little did I know it was a premonition for how I would be spending my mid-20s!

Ben Fankhauser

Davey

I first saw *Newsies* when I found out we were going to be doing a version of the movie at my summer camp. I was about eight or nine years old. My friends and I loved the movie, and I remember we all wanted to play Racetrack. I fell in love with acting through this camp. I loved that I got to be somebody else onstage. In this particular production, (this is terrible!) we added some random songs from other movie musicals. We had a set of girl twins, so the counselors aptly cast them as the Delancey "sisters." Bullies oftentimes feel lonely, and in our production the Delancey sisters sang "Out Here on My Own" from *Fame*. I played Crutchy and did the opening monologue that Max Casella does in the movie.

Michael Kosarin

stage music supervisor, vocal and incidental music arranger

Back in 1992, I saw a live-action Disney film called *Newsies*. While obviously flawed, it had an incredible score, and I became somewhat obsessed by the ballad "Santa Fe." Maybe not the best vocal in the world by Christian Bale, but who cared? It was fresh and exciting, with a phenomenal orchestration featuring a tasty harmonica solo and a big, open, Western sound. In those days before the Internet and YouTube, it required more work to be obsessed with recorded media, but I got a cassette tape of the film score and played the song many, many times, trying to figure out what made it tick. Why was it so appealing? Why was it not possible to get tired of listening to it? Why was this kid Christian Bale saying "muddah" instead of mother? I was already a big fan of Alan Menken's work, but didn't know Jack Feldman. Who was this guy, writing this incredibly clean, well-crafted theater lyric? I called my at-that-time new rep, Mark Sendroff, to see what he knew, and it turned out that Jack was his best pal. Mark connected me with Jack, as at that time I was still harboring dreams of writing the next great musical. We had a good time talking, but never agreed to write anything together. And so I had to be content to admire the writing of these two from afar, a newlywed in my Upper West Side apartment, playing the song over and over again. A few months later, I got a call from Alan Menken. Alan was looking for a music director for Disney Theatrical's first show ever—the stage production of *Beauty and the Beast*—and had heard from Danny Troob about my work as music director and arranger of the Broadway show *The Secret Garden*, which was just finishing its run. *Ahem.* I nervously drove up to Alan's house for an interview with him, and told him all about my love for his work, including his most recent at the time, *Newsies*. We hit it off, I got the job, and I've been his music director ever since.

"At first glance, it looks like something Disney must have locked away in a vault 25 years ago: a splashy, wide-screen, all-singing-all-dancing musical . . . with a cast of interchangeably bright-eyed, snub-nosed teenagers hoofing their way through studio sets and spouting G-rated wisecracks in their best show-biz-New York accents."

— OWEN GLEIBERMAN,
Entertainment Weekly
April 17, 1992

"I saw the movie at a Saturday morning preview attended by hundreds of children. . . . Although the material does indeed involve young protagonists, no effort is made to show their lives in a way today's kids can identify with."

— ROGER EBERT, *Chicago Sun-Times,* April 10, 1992

FANSIES

Shannon Prendergast, San Diego, CA

FANSIES

Darlene Slavick, Somerset, NJ

FANSIES

Michael Fatica, Cape Coral, FL

"*Newsies* taught me that you shouldn't be ashamed or scared of dancing and singing everywhere you go."

— Luke Saroni, Mesquite, TX

FANSIES

Jessica Sininger, Jacksonville, FL

"I met my friend Rachel in our freshman year of high school. I was new to the school and didn't know a single person. Rachel and I became fast friends when we both realized we had grown up watching *Newsies* and knew EVERY word. Fast-forward fifteen years, Rachel was living in New York and I was still in Omaha. I made the trip out, and as we sat in the theater, we both looked at each other with tears in our eyes. It was as if we never grew up. We were fifteen again and singing every single word. It is a memory I will forever hold dear to my heart."

— Mary Quinn, Omaha, NE

FANSIES

Ben Southerland, Dalton, GA

"My best friend introduced me to *Newsies* in 1992. We both loved musicals. Now my children watch it with me—they love when I sing the songs. It's now a tradition in our house."

— Shana Smith, Westminster, MD

Kate Reitz, Tampa, FL

Hannah Moors, Oceanside, CA

David Jacobs, Ocean Springs, MS

Nicole Zelka, Albany, NY

"I've been part of the *Newsies* fandom since 2001, in its heyday among online forums and fan groups. Being a part of this devoted community introduced me to some of my closest friends. And when we all came together to see the show on Broadway, for many of us, it was the first time we'd ever been in the same room together, the first time we were able to laugh and talk and bond in person. *Newsies* brought us together as teens, kept us together for over 10 years, and cemented our relationships as adults. Carryin' the banner, always."

— Jessica Osborne, Los Angeles, CA

Sarah Mariette, St. Paul, MN

"When I was little, *Newsies* was my security blanket. When kids were mean at school, these characters were my friends. The music and the story helped me to feel brave. It reminded me that sometimes things do work out for the underdog."

— Megan Robison, St. Louis, MO

Megan Robison, St. Louis, MO

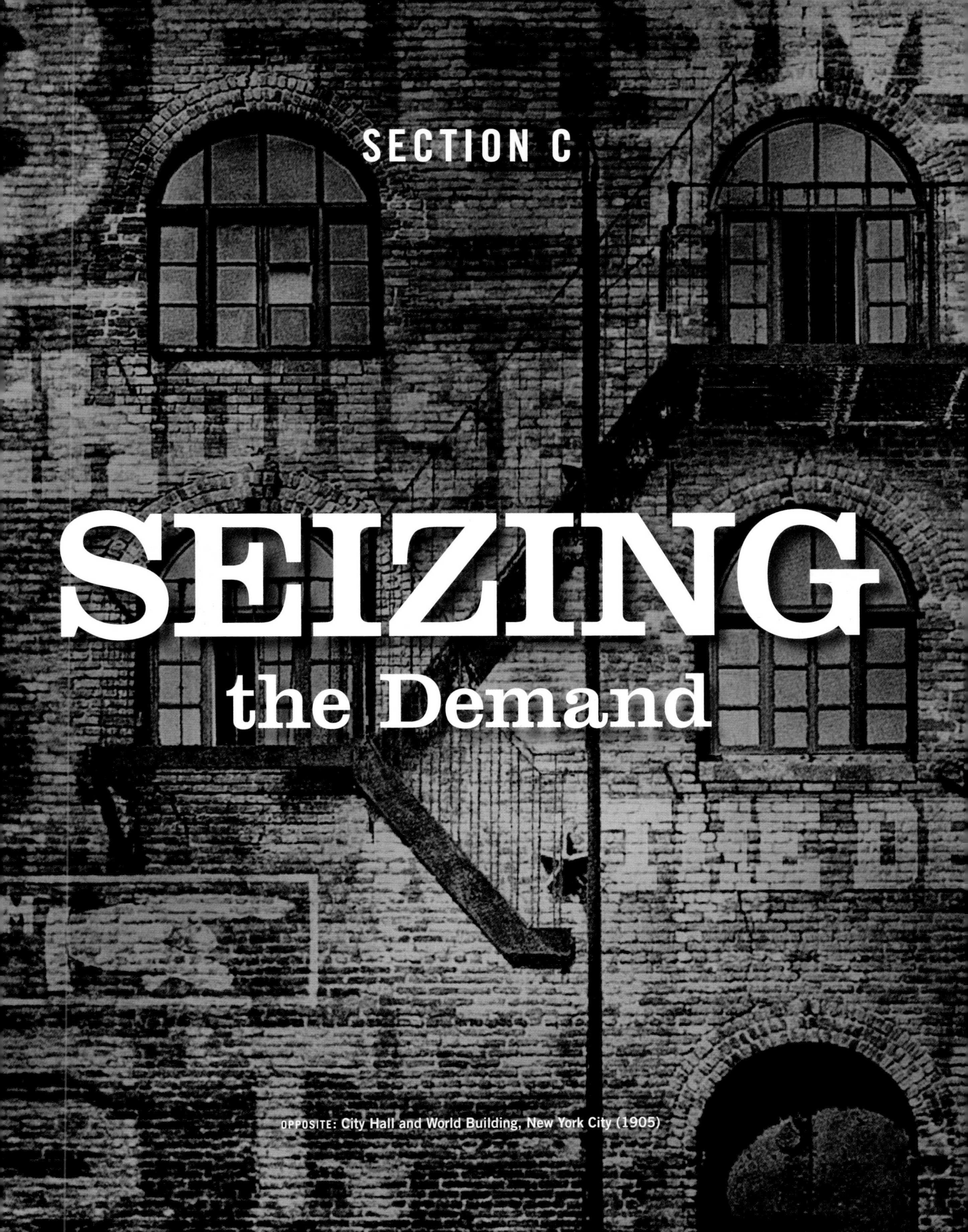

SECTION C

SEIZING the Demand

OPPOSITE: City Hall and World Building, New York City (1905)

Alan Menken, Jack Feldman, Harvey Fierstein

Coming Back to *Newsies*

Alan Menken

composer

The story of *Newsies* has been the most improbable journey, one that will forever serve as an inspiration to lost causes everywhere. We reached high with the movie, creating a break-into-song, live-action, honest-to-God movie musical. And then we watched it disappear overnight, with tepid reviews and nonexistent box office. On the very same night as I won two Oscars for *Beauty and the Beast*, I learned that *Newsies* had also won the Razzie Award for Worst Song of the Year. We were one of those famous disasters.

And then something happened. A generation of kids fell in love with this story and the songs that these newsboys sang. They watched it on video. They watched it on TV. They performed it at their schools and their camps, crafting scripts out of the movie dialogue and the songs. And, thank God, Disney Theatrical noticed. Fifteen years after the movie perished, I received a call about the plan to create a stage version of *Newsies* to release for stock and amateur productions. I was told that there was no need for me to do any additional work on it. Some writers would adapt the movie script and adjust our songs appropriately. Maybe some new songs would be added. But, since the idea was to simply counter all of the pirated versions that were circulating, I certainly had more important things to do with my time than to go to work on a stage adaptation of our under-appreciated little musical movie.

But there was no way I would let my baby be reworked by anyone else but Jack Feldman and me. And that decision set the stage for this little miracle now happening at the Nederlander Theatre on Broadway. Without any expectation of a first-class production, Jack, Noni White, Bob Tzudiker, and I embarked on the work of revisiting our characters and our story. And, when we were joined by an unstoppable, brilliant freight train named Harvey Fierstein as book writer, we completed a new, original, and fresh stage musical.

Noni White

Bob and I both thought *Newsies* would ultimately make a great stage musical. In fact, when we made our deal with Disney to write the film, we tried to retain the stage rights. Our lawyers at the time actually laughed at us, "It's your first deal, and it's with Disney. We'll never get that." At the time we didn't understand that our union, the Writers Guild of America, years before had won something called separated rights, which helped give us ownership of the story and characters we had created. But Disney would own the title (they had us change the film title to *Extra!* for a short time) and the music and lyrics. So Disney couldn't do a stage show without us, and we couldn't do it without them. But what better producer could we wish for? Although Disney never saw *Newsies* as Broadway-bound, mine was a different vision—I always said to Bob, "This can be huge . . . all-over-the-world huge."

Michael Kosarin

In October of 2008, I got a casual e-mail from Disney, asking if I was free to attend a private table reading of a stage version of an old Disney film called *Newsies*, as they were hoping to develop it for licensing and wanted me to arrange it. I sent an equally casual reply, saying that I was interested and could likely make it. (In an e-mail, no one can hear you scream.) But the reading was far from perfect. The wonderfully talented film scriptwriters had never written for the musical theater, which is a tremendously different medium requiring a different skill set. And the new opening song was a down-tempo affair called "Fallen Angels." (For the record, it contained this great internal rhyme by Jack Feldman: "Show every urchin/ there's a church in his heart where he may pray.") Everyone agreed that *Newsies* was not working as a stage show, and the idea was shelved. It was a personal disaster: I wasn't going to be able to work on the song "Santa Fe" after all. *Newsies* wasn't happening. Then, a few months later, enter theater legend Harvey Fierstein . . .

Harvey Fierstein

book writer

So, we were sitting around Alan Menken's studio wondering what project we could write together when I spotted the poster for *Newsies* on the wall. "How about a stage version of that?" I asked Alan. Having two nephews who grew up with the VHS tape, I'd seen the movie a bunch of times when babysitting. (Confession: I mostly paid attention to the scenes where the boys were dancing around or when the adorable teenaged Christian Bale was center screen, but I'd seen it.) Alan said, "Forget *Newsies*. We slaved over an adaptation. We even gave it two table readings. Disaster. It's never going to work. Forget it." I was hooked. There's nothing I like more than a challenge.

"Let me take a whack at it," I said. "I'll watch the movie again and see if there's something I can do to get it to work. If I come up with an idea, we can try. If not, no harm done." So, I watched the movie again and was immediately reminded of all of those terrific musical numbers: "Carrying the Banner," "Seize the Day," "Santa Fe," "The World Will Know" and the song that has always moved me most, "Once and For All." And then there were those dance numbers! Not since *Seven Brides for Seven Brothers* or *West Side Story* had there been the opportunity to showcase that brand of out-and-out joyful athleticism performed by a male ensemble. I was already imagining all of that energy exploding live from a Broadway stage.

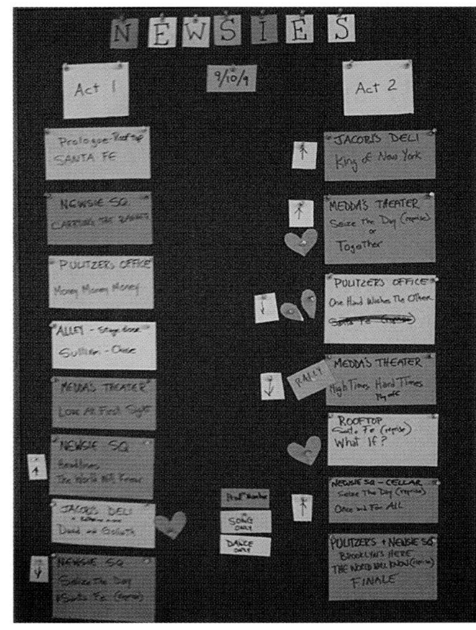

Early outline of the musical

Now, if I could just change the love story, deepen Jack Kelly's motivations, reinvent a few of the characters, and ditch some of the unnecessary baggage . . . I was ready to grab my computer and get to writing.

Suddenly I found myself in Disney Theatrical's magnificent offices high atop the New Amsterdam Theatre, meeting with its president, Tom Schumacher. "Harvey," he said with a smile, "if you could come up with a stage adaptation, you would make a lot of people happy. *Newsies* is our most requested title for production by high schools, colleges, community theaters, and summer camps. We've always had to turn them down. But if you could fashion a version we could provide them . . ." Again I found myself saying, "Let me try. The worst that could happen is that Alan, Jack Feldman (our more-than-willing lyricist), and I waste some time."

Michael Kosarin

Harvey was full of ideas on how to successfully make the show transfer to the stage, but his two biggest ones right off the bat were: 1) change the newspaper writer—who had been played by Bill Pullman in the film—into a young woman who would be Jack Kelly's love interest, and 2) start the show with the song "Santa Fe." The show would start with "Santa Fe"?!? I knew then that we'd be a hit.

Do-Over!

Jack Feldman

lyricist

Writing the stage version of *Newsies* was a singularly satisfying experience for me in many ways. For starters, I was collaborating with Alan and Harvey, and we had a blast. And then there's this: we were getting the almost unheard-of opportunity for a do-over. When Alan and I wrote the score for the movie, which opened (and very quickly closed) in 1992, short deadlines and the prerecording of songs before filming left little time for rewrites. I was sure every lyric could have been better, but at a certain point I knew that ship had sailed. In the years since, new audiences embraced the movie on cable, VHS and DVD, and Disney Theatrical decided to develop a stage version for licensing. I couldn't believe it: do-over!

Some lyrics had to be rewritten because a song's function and placement had changed (e.g., "Santa Fe"). We also wrote new songs for new characters (e.g., Katherine), and replaced old songs that no longer belonged (e.g., "My Lovey-Dovey Baby"). As for the rest, I grabbed the chance to go back and make improvements in any number of areas: clarity, storytelling, character, gracefulness, etc. Here are a couple of examples:

FILM:

We need a good assassination!
We need an earthquake or a war!
How 'bout a crooked politician?
Hey, stupid, that ain't news no more!

STAGE:

You wanna sell the next edition?
Give us a earthquake or a war!
How 'bout a crooked politician?
Ya nitwit, that ain't news no more!

The point of those lines is to help define character by emphasizing the kids' street smarts and cynicism. I don't remember why I didn't rhyme the word "politician" back then, because rhyming a word helps it stand out, and "crooked politician" is what sets up the next line. Finding a replacement line that rhymed wasn't hard. There was nothing wrong with "an earthquake," but I like "a earthquake" better because it sounds wrong in the right way: it's unexpected without sacrificing clarity, and it tells us something about the kids' social class. And "Ya nitwit" is just technically easier to sing than "Hey, stupid."

FILM:

And the time is now,
And the winds will blow.

STAGE:

And a roar will rise
From the streets below.

"The time is now" is not only self-evident, but I'd used the line earlier in the song and it was a waste of words the first time; maybe I was hoping it would improve with age. "And the winds will blow": what does that even mean? Of course the winds will blow—that's pretty much what winds do. If I'd meant the winds of change, I should have said so, except I shouldn't have because there are few clichés more tired than that one.

Luckily, many people who are loyal to the movie have been very accepting of these and other changes, with one glaring exception. The verse I'm referring to was extraneous, misleading, overwrought and silly, but in spite of this—or, let's face it, because of this—the loss of it has caused much anger and grief. I am of course referring to the section of "Carrying the Banner" known as "Patrick's Mother." Guys, please forgive me and take comfort in knowing that it will always be there on the soundtrack, haunting me until the day I die.

Professionally speaking, it was very satisfying to make my work better. Personally, though, nothing was as moving to me as the conversations I had with a number of the young actors who told me that it was the movie of *Newsies* that gave them the courage to go to dance class—a socially risky and possibly dangerous decision for a boy even today—and dare to dream of a career in the arts. In a journey filled with so many happy surprises, it's these moments I'll cherish the most.

No doubt there are still lyrics in *Newsies* that could be better, but the last thing I want is another do-over. In fact, when all is said and done, I wouldn't want to change a thing.

The Developmental Readings

Justin Huff

Fast-forward past college and many years performing at Walt Disney World to my career as a casting director in New York City. It wasn't until after a few years and casting many Broadway shows that my dream came true. In the summer of 2009, we received a call at Telsey + Company that Disney was thinking of developing *Newsies* for the stage and wanted to know if our office would cast the first developmental reading. This could be my chance to be a part of *Newsies* and help bring this story and music to a whole new generation! I instantly jumped at the chance to be a part of the process.

Jeff Lee

staff associate director, DTG

When looking for the right rehearsal space for the first developmental reading in May 2010, we considered all the usual-suspect studios in New York City's Theater District but instead selected Ballet Hispanico all the way uptown on West 89th Street. In their larger ballet room near the top floor, the two side walls are all windows, and you were high enough to look across the rooftops of the Upper West Side of Manhattan—a live backdrop for several scenes in the show, which created a great rehearsal atmosphere. Most Disney shows feature environments that are either fantasy or halfway around the world for which nobody has any point of reference. But here we were in New York, developing a show that's set in New York—albeit 111 years earlier. Some of the young actors we hired recently got off a bus or a plane from somewhere else in the country and didn't really have a feeling of Manhattan yet. So they were kind of living it for the first time (in both 1899 and 2010) as we rehearsed.

My goal in directing developmental readings is to illuminate the written ma-

Disney

NEWSIES!

THE STAGE MUSICAL

Music by Alan Menken
Lyrics by Jack Feldman
Book by Harvey Fierstein

Based on the Disney film
written by Bob Tzudiker & Noni White

29-Hour Reading Presentation

Ballet Hispanico

Friday, May 14, 2010
2:30 PM

terial rather than present a staging or production concept. We take the words and notes on the page—the story that is being told and the music that supports that story—and give it some life.

Luckily, at Disney we don't have the pressure of selling a show to anyone with an open checkbook like at a normal backers' audition, so it's all about seeing whether or not the material works. If you encounter a scene or a relationship or a song placement that isn't working, you either fix it on the spot, juggle things around if you can, or do your best to give the actors some sort of inspiration and motivation to make what we have on paper work.

The cast was great, and the energy in the room was amazing. There is always a lot of work to get done, but it was a lot of fun. And we actually did more development work with Alan and Jack and Harvey than I've ever experienced in a reading. They really got their hands dirty—and were excited about it! With a show of this energy level, sitting at a bunch of music stands and standing up when it is your turn to talk wasn't going to give the unique material a fair representation, no matter how great the actors sounded or how well they understood the story. So I added more legit staging than what I might normally do in one of these readings, just to give it some support. But then the actors got so into it; we had to pull them back a bit. The staging really got in the face of everyone sitting on the other side of the table, which was deliberate.

The great thing about Jeremy Jordan was that he walked in the room and he was Jack. Everything that came out of his mouth was pitch-perfect. There was an energy about him that you didn't want to mess with. It was kind of a wonderful mystery. You hear these stories about actors who work on film, wonderful actors who live the entire shoot of the movie as the character, whether they are at the food truck or in their trailer or in front of the camera. It felt that way with Jeremy. He didn't need to do anything. He would just sit, look you in the eye, listen, digest—rarely was there ever any question, rarely was there ever any challenge—then do it back. And it was there. That's kind of eerie, but it was also refreshing because you don't have much time and he just did it!

Theresa Bailey

production stage manager, first reading

After having worked on several Disney productions over the years—including *Beauty and the Beast*, *The Lion King*, and *The Little Mermaid*—I was honored to be asked to stage-manage the first professional reading of *Newsies*. One of my favorite memories was a day that Alan, Harvey, and Jack were discussing rewriting "The Story of My Life" for Katherine, played by Jennifer Damiano, who has a very distinctive voice and character. After several creative sessions, Alan turned to Jack and asked excitedly, "So are the new lyrics ready?" Jack retorted with a bit of steam, "It's not that simple, you know. The words don't just appear out of nowhere. These things take time. It doesn't happen in five minutes!" Alan replied, "For me it does . . . I just go into a room and a few minutes later come out with some music." A moment of silence, then the entire room broke into laughter.

Veteran actor Patrick Page was Pulitzer for this reading. Andrew Keenan-Bolger (Crutchie) and Jason Michael Snow (Davey) were among his many admirers in the young cast. And there was a dynamic chemistry between Patrick and Jeremy that really gave life to their characters. Speaking of chemistry, there was a kiss between Katherine and Jack in the second act, but both Jennifer and Jeremy were saving that element for later in rehearsals. Since there really wasn't much time, they had many discussions about the beats leading up to the kiss and then how long it would be and who would break the kiss and so on and so on. But one day during the scene, they accidentally got carried away and actually kissed, which surprised them, and then they just started laughing, which, of course, made everyone else laugh. Our cast had great energy, which got the reading audience excited. It was clear that *Newsies* had legs.

Danny Troob

I was far from delighted when I heard about the stage show. Another chance to fail! But I went to a reading of the new script that Harvey Fierstein had crafted, with Jeremy Jordan reading the part of Jack, I realized instantly that things could be very different with the stage show. Harvey had neatly solved all the problems with the story while keeping room for all the best songs from the movie. And Jeremy, well, Jeremy was a star . . .

Chris Montan

I think we would have just been making a better version of the movie if Harvey hadn't come aboard. You needed someone who wouldn't hold on to any one particular element if it was hurting us. When you think of all the musical-comedy-friendly elements that Harvey added, they really made it a stage show. Creating the main character of Katherine—a sparring partner and love interest for Jack—was huge. And it made Jack smarter to have a smart girlfriend. Because we didn't have any romance in the movie (Jack's spark with Davey and Les's sister Sarah, a secondary character, was minor). And a musical comedy without romance really has a gun to its head. We still have the history there, we have the rebellion of the children, but it's in a more proper balance. And the romance doesn't overtake the piece, which is about young men dancing and singing viscerally. If you take what is entertaining about *Newsies* at its core, it is those boys doing "Carrying the Banner" or "King of New York." It's thrilling.

Jeff Lee

There was a good amount of musical material reworked or rewritten for the second reading in December 2010, which we did across the street from our New Amsterdam Theatre offices at the New 42nd Street Studios. The primary song for Pulitzer was constantly a topic of conversation, and we ended up going through a few different options before landing on something. Katherine used to sing "The Story of My Life," which many of us loved, but "Watch What Happens" ultimately had a better energy and a better narrative. We tried to figure out when and how the guys from Brooklyn should show up, and how to split up the cast in the second act so that in the absence of costumes the audience wouldn't be confused that the same actors were playing newsies from a different borough. We started to look at the functions of secondary older characters for efficiencies. Some cast changes helped illuminate developing characters. For example, our two Pulitzers, Patrick Page and Shuler Hensley—two completely different actors and two completely different types—are both brilliant, and either could have ultimately done the role onstage.

The hardest part of the development process for me is getting excited about a show. As it moves into production, I don't necessarily move with it because a separate creative team becomes attached. So I watch it grow and come to life—proud of it and supportive of it—but not necessarily as contributive as I would like to be. It's like the nanny giving back the baby at the end of the day. But to be there at its birthing place is something to be remembered.

Eduardo Castro

Early on when I was working on *Tarzan* in 2005, there was a rumor, or at least a dream, of *Newsies* actually becoming a stage production. But I didn't really pay much attention to it until five years later, when I was asked to help out with contracts for the second *Newsies* reading. It was a thrilling opportunity to do something new at Disney and to see it from the start. And the fact that it was *Newsies*...! Once we got into rehearsals and heard the music come alive with the performers, that's when you started getting the chills. And you're like, "Oh, my God, this could be AMAZING. This could really be what everybody has been talking about for years!" And then we finished, because it was just a week. I just said, "Okay, I have to keep the excitement a little bit down just in case it doesn't go anywhere." But I truly felt that this was going to go . . . there had to be something else to it.

Chris Montan

The score got better and better as we shaped it for the stage. For 20 years I'd been saying to Alan, "I want to have five more 'King of New York's," because that song came in late to the film when I had been pushing for another big song with a great hook. As good as it was, the trouble with the film score was that it was a little bit too monochromatic. You know, "The World Will Know," "Seize the Day" . . . all the big anthem songs. We needed to vary it for the stage, and I think a lot of what we added, like Pulitzer's song and Katherine's song and the love song, just changed the balance of the score so that it wasn't just anthems. Going into the stage adaptation, I guess I was a little gun-shy, because I had gone through the movie's failure. We work as hard on the ones that don't last as the ones that do. But once we had Katherine and changed the dynamics and added all these new songs, it sure felt good.

Alan Menken

After the second reading, the idea of maybe thinking beyond going directly to licensing hit everyone all at once. Could we mount a limited run of the show to kick off releasing it? And wheels began to turn. Expectations had to be managed. It was a balancing act of extraordinary proportions. And no one does that with more skill than Tom Schumacher.

Ashley Carpenter, Galloway, NJ

Aimee Weyrauch, Orlando, FL

Erin Elliott, Peoria, IL

Tess McDermott, Guelph, Canada

"Growing up as a dancer, *Newsies* was my favorite musical to watch, sing along with and choreograph to, particularly "King of New York." I have a huge appreciation for all the hard work that goes into making a production come to life on stage."

— Tess McDermott, Guelph, Canada

"*Newsies* is remarkable because it is a story about underdogs. It's a story about people, young adults, who find themselves in a world that doesn't believe they matter. Everybody in the audience has had a moment when they feel like they don't matter. The newsies remind us that we, as individual people, can make a difference. It is a story about us."

— Stephanie Mendoza, Houston, TX

Megan O'Neill, Pittsburgh, PA

"The way the show is written and executed doesn't tug on your heartstrings, but yanks them. You can tell everyone has put their tears, blood, and sweat into it."

— Harley Kulp, Orlando, FL

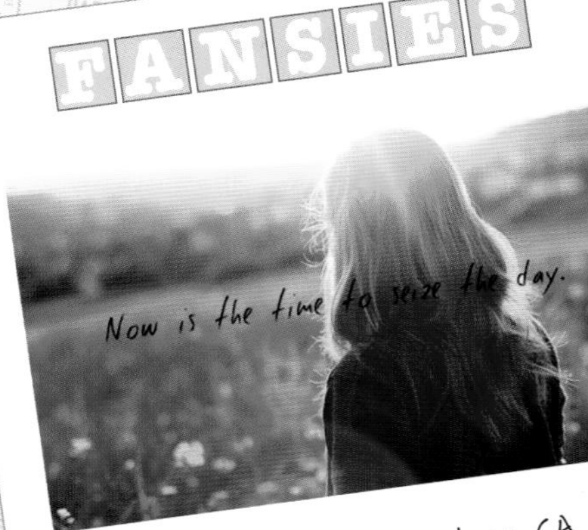

Megan Clancy, Pasadena, CA

Rebecca Pruitt, Fresno, CA

Keely O'Connor, Fairfax, VA

Kayla Follett, Litchfied, NH

"*Newsies* is a prime example of what every Broadway musical should be. Its classic and catchy songs, unbelievably choreographed numbers, and overall high energy leaves the audience smiling night after night. There's something magical about it."

— Wendi Reichstein, Houston, TX

Heather O, MN

"Being a theater kid in my country is not all that common or easy, and this musical has definitely inspired me to chase my dreams no matter how complicated they seem. It has also taught me that if you think something's wrong with your environment, don't be afraid. Take a stand and change it, because no matter how small or insignificant we may appear, we can ALL make a difference!"

— Karin Trejo, Mexico City, Mexico

"I started a fan site (NewsiesFreak.com) where I was able to spread my love for this movie to the world. I signed many petitions hoping to get *Newsies* on Broadway, but never thought my dream would actually come true!"

— Jennifer Sothy, Anaheim, CA

Jennifer Sothy, Anaheim, CA

The World

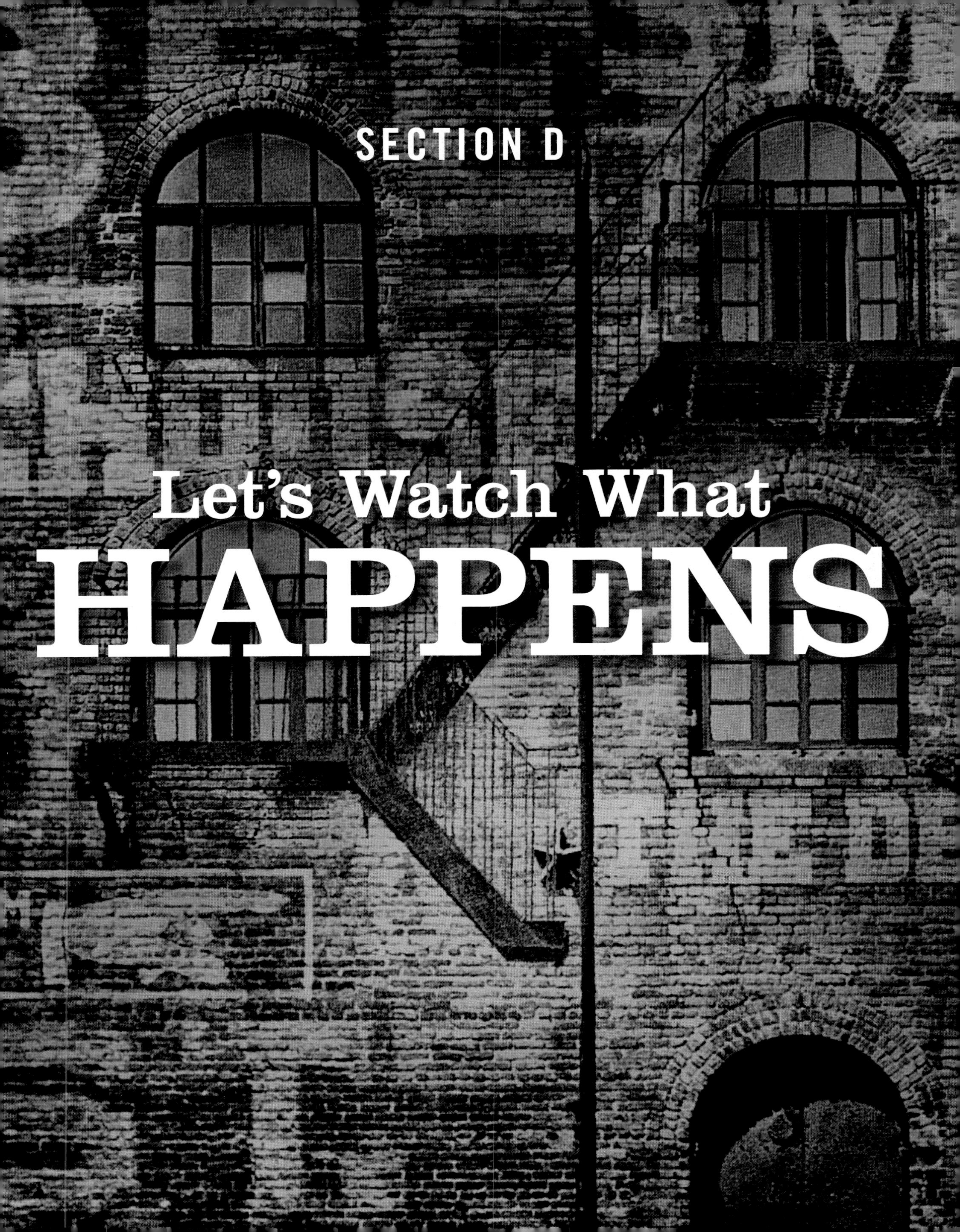

SECTION D

Let's Watch What HAPPENS

The "Yes" That Changed Everything

Mark Hoebee
artistic director, Paper Mill Playhouse

The very first time I heard about *Newsies* was in 2002. Someone—it might have been Michael Gennaro, the former CEO here—said, "Do you know about this Disney movie? It's a great project that I think could be made into a stage show." So I watched it and loved the whole spirit of it—loved the music, obviously, and all the choreography. It is about youthful enthusiasm. After Michael initially reached out to Disney, the project sort of fell away. I forgot about it, as we do when we get wrapped up in other things. And then my son, who was eight years old, discovered the movie and wanted to buy the DVD. He started watching it in the car all the time so it stayed in the back of my mind.

Then I met Steve Fickinger, who was heading Disney's theatrical licensing business, while I was directing *High School Musical*. He came and saw it and was really happy with it, so we kept in touch. A few years later, he called and said, "I have a project, and I want to talk to you about it. Would you come in?" I didn't know what it was. And when he started talking about *Newsies*, immediately my eyes lit up and I thought, "I cannot believe that we are having this conversation!" He said, "We're looking for a home to test it. Is this something you'd be interested—" I didn't let him finish. "YES. Absolutely, yes! I know the raw material; it is perfectly suited to our audience, and I'd love to work with Disney on a new project." I was thrilled, even before I turned the first page.

I went hard to work with our team, including Mimi Intagliata, our Director of Production. We had a bunch of meetings to see if we could make it work; then we came to an agreement that, yes, we could make a production happen here. And I was over the moon. At the time, we were under sort of a confidentiality agreement with Steve and Disney that we weren't going to talk about it, which was fine. So we would have these big covert conversations here at Paper Mill—and we had a code name: The Hush-Hush Project. We would always say we have to talk about "Hush Hush," and people would look at us oddly because they didn't know what we were talking about. I was bound and determined not to leak a word of it until we agreed we were going to move forward with it. But once we got the green light, I started to get really excited.

Paper Mill Playhouse, Millburn, NJ

Creating a Production with Heart

Jeff Calhoun
director

The definitive word that comes to mind when I reflect on the *Newsies* experience is "heart"! Like the newsboys' triumph over Pulitzer and his world of greed and capitalism, our creative team's triumph over the enormous odds of commercial success is a story of beating the odds and touching the heart. What a "dream team" I had to work with: Harvey, Alan, Jack, and Chris. Whether discussing music at Alan's estate beneath his myriad of Oscars and Grammys, talking text at Harvey's fabulous fun house museum of a home, or sitting with Chris at my kitchen table storyboarding each dance and transition, their generosity of spirit exemplified true collaboration.

That same spirit of collaboration extended to our entire design team. One of the many challenges for a director is to create a physical production that honors and supports the text, music, and lyrics of a show. In accomplishing this I had world-class help. Jess Goldstein and Chuck LaPointe captured the tone of the late 1800s with their impeccable costume, hair, and makeup designs. Sven Ortel and Jeff Croiter enhanced the storytelling by elegantly painting with projections and lighting. And, always wanting the set to be another character in the musical, I called on my "secret weapon," set designer Tobin Ost.

After reading the script, we decided that at times the set would need to be Goliath to the boys' David, a vertical

Model designs for the towers set by Tobin Ost

cityscape meant to dwarf and intimidate, and at other times it would represent the city's obstacles that the boys must scale and traverse to escape trouble—all while creating cinematic scene changes. It was this stage direction that most informed us about how the set would need to function: *(JACK, DAVEY, and LES leap up onto a fire escape ladder and take off. The COP and SNYDER try to follow. The set turns as the BOYS climb over the roof and back down the other side, into the alley of a burlesque house.)*

It was clear from the turntable reference that Harvey knew that the set must be able to "dance." Although we didn't feel like this was a show that necessarily needed to revolve, it did inspire us to create three impressive towers that could gracefully slide, turn, and morph into whatever architecture the script called for. One of my favorite marriages between the set and the text happens in

act two when the newsboys create and execute a plan to distribute their underground newspaper. They are feeling on top of the world as they get their word out to every corner of each borough during "Once and For All." I get goose bumps every time I see the boys infiltrate all three levels of the set, creating a phalanx of metal and humanity as the towers slowly move downstage.

NEWSIES BANNER
NEWSIES BANNER
NEWSIES BANNER
NEWSIES BANNER
NEWSIES BANNER

Circulation Books
District-Attorney

Scenery That Dances

Tobin Ost
set designer

"Being boss doesn't mean you have all the answers. Just the brains to recognize the right one when you hear it." This line of Katherine's perfectly captures our creative collaboration. The notion of bringing the late 19th century to life onstage came in phases, with crucial input and feedback from many creative people. If theater is truly collaborative, then what we collectively experienced as we got *Newsies* on its feet epitomized this idea.

The initial impulse for the set design was to provide a space that reflected a straightforward and relatively "real" feeling for the story that was written—after all, the events in *Newsies* are modeled after an actual event that took place in 1899, and the script moves in a very cinematic, linear sort of way. Consequently, I came up with a scheme that demonstrated storefronts, building façades, and other unmistakable locations through which the newsies could move. Perspective was forced in such a way as to emphasize how small these kids were in relation to the not-so-sympathetic city that towered over them.

Director Jeff Calhoun and I worked through this concept with a series of rough sketches and a ground plan. Although it was very early in the process, we presented our fledgling thoughts to Tom Schumacher. It was one of the best—and most formative—things that happened in the process of figuring out the set design. Contrary to my own preconceived notions, it turned that out Tom was not at all interested in realizing a "yesteryear" sort of design; he wanted us to move our ideas out of the literal and staid and into something that would be exciting to a young, contemporary audience. I left the meeting with my small pile of chicken-scratch sketches and a few ideas that still felt like what we ultimately wanted to say. The scale of the environment—something that could dwarf the newsies—was still very important to everyone.

Early set design sketch by Tobin Ost

Another defining concept came to the forefront, which both Tom and Jeff at different times had mentioned in this seminal meeting: that of the set being a "jungle gym." The prior idea for the set, while cosmetically providing height with tall pieces of scenery, avoided levels except for one sequence during which Jack, Davey, and Les run from Snyder through the streets and alleys of Manhattan and take refuge in the backstage of Miss Medda Larkin's theater. Harvey Fierstein had written this ambitious and harrowing segment of the script, and Tom had caught this singular level change in what we had devised to that point. Suddenly, the thought became less about a set that had a jungle gym in it and more about a jungle gym that had a set in it. It supported what Jeff had wanted in being able to tell the story quite literally on many levels—providing both practical levels for the newsies to utilize as well as metaphorical levels in terms of the ideas of class and social standing of the "Davids versus the Goliaths" in this particular world.

As this "jungle gym" idea began to emerge, it became clear that in order to demonstrate New York and the sheer scale that had unilaterally been deemed so important, the levels of this "jungle gym" had to carry as high as possible onstage. It also became clear that we needed to be able to demonstrate intimacy within this structure and allow enough space to support what was promised to be some very athletic and explosive dancing sequences choreographed by Chris Gattelli. This would not be overly successful with a static structure; so instead of requiring the actors to accommodate its location, why not have it accommodate theirs? And so I began to think of the jungle gym as something that not only moved, but moved in such a way that it could get out of the way for major dance sequences or be in the faces of the front row for smaller, more intimate scenes.

I developed a small, rough model and showed it to Jeff. Within five minutes of moving the pieces around, it became innately clear that the new idea was going to work. I had already devised several "broad stroke" positions for the pieces of the jungle gym (at this point referred to more and more as the "towers"), but in Jeff's hands the variation and variety of exactly how these could be used became wonderfully apparent. With his thoughts behind this new idea, the towers were not only moving, they were quite literally dancing and becoming integral to every beat of the score.

The set and the blocking became inseparable, and as we moved page to page through the script and vetted the towers in Jeff's uptown apartment, we began to look for how to make the different locations even more tailored and specific. We also knew that making 24-foot-tall metal towers move effortlessly was a very tall order to begin with, and for as quickly as they might actually be able to move, the actors in a chase sequence would still be quicker.

It also became clear that, apart from how these towers ultimately moved, the solution to "keeping up" with the speedy pace of the script, music, and blocking was not to be found in a profusion of other built scenic pieces heaped into the picture but perhaps in projected imagery. It could also move, sometimes along with the towers and sometimes purposely against it; it could move fast and provide its own excitement to scenic changes; it could be bombastic and aggressive, or it could be delicate and subtle; it could be expansive and support an enormous group number or isolated to help anchor a single actor. It could also be malleable and change with the writing as it developed—this was still very early in the process and we wanted to be able to flex with the writers as the final script came into focus.

Ryan Breslin

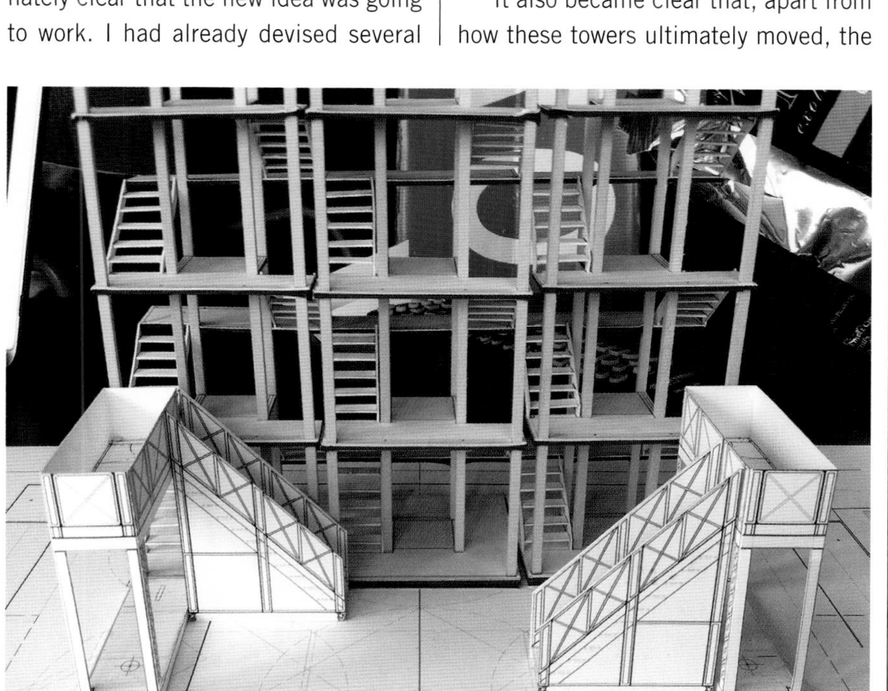

Early model design for the tower set

The towers received a series of scrim panels printed with a crinkled paper texture so that if they were ever seen without projection, they would still be interesting to look at. These became another major key in landing the final design because these panels, like the towers themselves, moved—and moved quickly. They were designed to roll or unroll as the scene and the projected images dictated. We could have all of the panels unrolled and the towers positioned in such a way to create a projection surface that filled the entire stage, or we could have only one open to create a minor location or moment.

Projection designer Sven Ortel came on board and through his own insights of how to elegantly suggest location and the overall spirit of the material, we finally had the pieces assembled that we collectively felt would best deliver the story of *Newsies*. Other scenic elements and props were peppered into this concept, but only with economy, when it truly felt like something was missing or couldn't be told in a satisfying way with the towers and projections alone.

Lighting designer Jeff Croiter worked in tandem with these ideas and, given the skeletal nature of the towers as well as the important technical balance of light levels with Sven's projection brightness, was able to sculpt phenomenal locations and specificity that were as essential to the architecture of the look as either set or projections.

In short, I'd say the very best moments of the *Newsies* set design are when the blocking, sets, projections, and lighting are seamless, when the lines blur between where one leaves off and another picks up. Each area has distinct moments that come to the forefront, but it's the tailored, collaborative balance between them all that makes it feel singular. And I think this is what collaboration truly is: a balancing act of bringing thoughts and ideas to the table, but also knowing when to get the hell out of the way! Or, in Jeff Calhoun's words, "Let the best idea win."

Making the Towers Viable

Anne Quart
associate producer and
vice president of production, DTG

Although I had been working on *The Lion King* for a decade, I had just started to head all of production in 2011, which was a very busy year at Disney Theatrical. We all knew that the pilot production of *Aladdin* at Seattle's 5th Avenue Theatre in early summer was going to take some energy, but for some reason I had in my head that *Newsies* at Paper Mill Playhouse later in the year was just going to mount itself. Then I remember very clearly standing in the lobby of the 5th Avenue on the phone with Paper Mill's Mimi Intagliata and Mark Hoebee, grappling with the budget: they had this much money, and we had this much money, but Tobin's inspired set design, which Tom had fallen in love with, was going to cost half a million dollars more than we had budgeted to build. You couldn't cut half a million dollars out of that set and have anything left! So we were faced with going back to Tom, then returning to Jeff and Tobin to come up with something vastly cheaper . . . or figuring out a way to make this design viable.

Cast touring the towers at Hudson Scenic, Yonkers, NY

With three big towers that come downstage and rotate to create various atmospheres, you couldn't just go to one tower—it's not quite the same. There was just no way to make cuts without bastardizing everything they came up with. So I thought, "Well, what if we built it so it could tour?" Because the whole point of *Newsies*, although no one believes us, was for it to go direct to licensing. And until opening night at Paper Mill, I also believed that 100%. Building the set to tour was not about our secret plan to move it to Broadway or to put it on the road. It was about how we could build it so that we could ultimately rent it to various licensing partners and make back our investment. That is what I sold to Tom: "What if we spent about $250,000 to $300,000 more than our current projected deficit and built it to tour? We could rig up those towers on chain motors, put the deck in underneath it, drop the towers down, and you could do the show. For licensing partners, the set could move and go up pretty quickly. We could rent it to Tuacahn, rent it to the Muny, rent it to the Ahmanson . . . and I bet in two, three, four rentals, we'd make back our investment. We could send people a *Newsies* package based on what we did at Paper Mill." I didn't present an alternative—there just wasn't one, other than a wing-and-drop show. I remember sitting in the house of the 5th Avenue with Tom sitting down right in front of me. "I'm gonna go to David with this." And he said, "Absolutely, that is what we have to do." To his credit, David Schrader (our executive vice president and managing director—the money guy) went, "I get it." And it happened pretty quickly. It all boiled down to what we could do to protect the design, which we all knew was special.

Painting with Projections

Sven Ortel
projection designer

When I was asked to meet with Jeff and Tobin to discuss the use of projections on *Newsies*, I had very little knowledge of the source material and knew nothing about what they wanted to do with the show. I had watched the movie the night before and read a little book about street kids in turn-of-the-20th-century New York. Since I occupy myself with creating imagery and integrating it into shows, having seen the movie was very important, not so much in terms of storytelling but in terms of the visual style. And I do like paying homage to source material in my work.

ABOVE: Brooklyn Bridge set projection. BELOW: Collage by Sven Ortel

What Tobin and Jeff presented to me was a model box with the essence of what constitutes the stage set we have today: the three towers, two wagons, and light boxes on the side and the back. They wanted the towers to have three screens each on one side that scroll down to create different configurations and thus help to evoke the place and period of the action when imagery is projected onto them. It sounds simple enough, but as with most simple-sounding ideas, the execution is far from it. During the meeting, Tobin just moved the scaled-down versions of the towers around with his hands to illustrate the different configurations. It dawned on me that the imagery, whatever it may be, would have to "travel" with those towers and screens wherever they go, appear when the screens scroll down,

and disappear when they move up. That was the major technical challenge of the design, because I knew this just had to work and look effortless in order to support the show. Luckily, cutting-edge technology and a team of talented, smart people helped me to make that part happen somewhat unnoticed, and that was precisely the goal. In 1899, the term "modern technology" was associated with inventions such as the fountain pen, the vacuum flask, and the zipper—not projections that follow tracking towers around.

The development of artwork had a different journey. I had to ask myself, "How do I create imagery in 2011 that evokes 1899?" Tobin gave me a great cue early on, because he had already created artwork for the light boxes in a palette of inky greens and blues, and I loved that palette of colors. However, I also wanted everything to look authentic and hand-made, or rather, hand-printed. Whilst I was doing a lot of research into the actual locations of the events described in the book (newspaper row, newsboys lodgings, tenement buildings on the Lower East Side), I experimented with printing-press effects on photos my team and I took of brick walls at various locations around New York. These treated new photos I tried to combine with historical photos, then layered period newspaper clippings and typefaces over them. In order to present these ideas, I mocked up what the imagery would look like if it were projected onto the set.

That step of the process was crucial because the projections and the set were always intended to be a unified whole. For that to be true, other elements had to be thoroughly researched and created as well: the typefaces used had to be historically correct, and, crucially, the physical *Newsies Banner* had to be the same one that is shown in the printing-press video sequence. This part of the design was intended as homage to the movie, and thus it is also the most cinematic. We found a working historical printing-press business in the Brooklyn Navy Yard (Woodside Press, a veritable printing-press museum), and they allowed us to film the process of making the banner from start to finish. We picked type and set it, cut historical newspaper paper to size, applied ink to an old letterpress, and then went on to print about 50 *Newsies Banners* by hand after the printing plate was fixed down. Of course, we had to make an actual *Newsies Banner* printing plate first. This is probably my favorite memento of that great day when we printed the banner. The prop used in the show is an enlarged version of the banner we printed that day. The resulting footage was treated with inky colors and textures to age it and make it gel with the rest of the imagery, set, and lighting, and finally edited to work with the rhythm of "Once and For All."

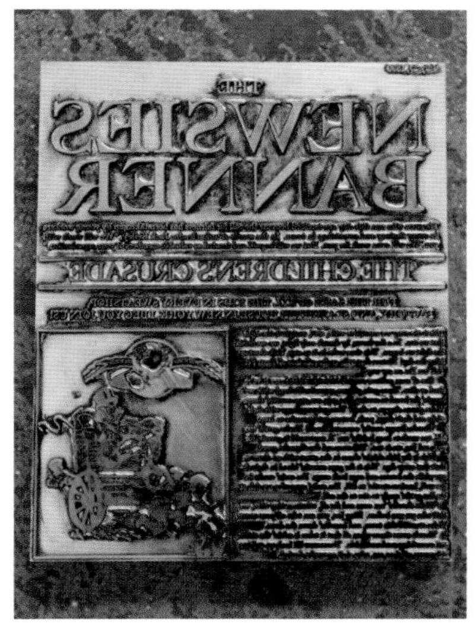

The Newsies Banner printing plate

he men who run this city are
every factory and sweatshop
ou. We will even work for you.

THE
VS ES
ecause the call for fairness een taken up by young worke
In the words of union lea ack Kelly, "We will work wit
l be paid and treated as va e members of your organization
DREN'S RUSADE

Lighting with Edge

Jeff Croiter
lighting designer

I was not one of the huge fans of the movie. I liked it—it was great—but I was not someone who saw it 12 times. I got the call from Michele Steckler at Disney, with whom I had been working on *Peter and the Starcatcher*, probably about four months before the Paper Mill production. "Would you be interested in being a part of *Newsies*? No guarantees, but Paper Mill mentioned your name, Jeff Calhoun mentioned your name, and, of course, your name has come up here as well. So if it is something you are interested in—" My response: "Absolutely! When is it?" She told me the dates, and I said, "I want to do it, but I would need to know very soon so I can tell someone else I'm not available," and the next day I got an offer. That is how it happened. Tobin and I had done a few shows together through the years; he did costumes on one or two and sets on another. And Jeff and I had done one show at Ars Nova that was a lot of fun.

A couple of months before we started at Paper Mill, Jeff invited me to his apartment on the Upper West Side. Tobin was there, and we sat down with their rough set model and he talked through the whole show. Without telling me any lighting-specific ideas, he explained how the set would function and how he saw the show conceptually and visually. That was before projections were involved. For several weeks, and even after I met Sven, I had no idea what the projection element was going to be, which could change everything I do drastically, as lighting would do more work on the set if there were no projections. I approach lighting a show from a storytelling point of view—trying to help the audience feel something or see something or understand something better than they would have without light-

Jeff Croiter during technical rehearsals

ing. Projections can enhance that because they put a literal texture up on the stage. Working hand in hand with the projectionist to tell the story is essential because these two elements only work well if they work together. At a certain point before we got to Paper Mill, I knew what Sven was doing, because I could see images, but he didn't really know what I was doing. We had the most dialogue when we were in tech together. Once he started seeing my colors and the textures I was using on the actors, we were able to work together to make something cohesive. Sometimes projections stand out as an element that doesn't fit in a production, but in *Newsies* they mesh very well.

Tobin's towers posed unique challenges. If I were lighting a musical with actors who stood on the floor, I would light one plane—the floor—upstage to downstage, left to right, the floor being the 0-0 point. With *Newsies*, not only are the towers really tall with three levels, but they could go anyplace we wanted them to go. We had to light upstage to downstage, left to right, *and* top to bottom—the entire volume of the space. Even in a show like *Peter Pan*, where people are flying around, there is a follow-spot on the one person or two people flying. This was a group of 20 boys running all over this place! So we had to figure out a way to be flexible yet economical.

After I knew I was doing *Newsies*, I walked around New York City, and every time I saw light passing through anything that looked like a city structure, I took a picture of it. I didn't do a lot of library photo research because it is all right here. As you walk around many neighborhoods in New York, light going through fire escapes is no different now than it was in 1899. So that fueled the fire. I still have picture after picture of different kinds of shadows that the city makes. We used the towers to re-create some of those shadows, but we also had shadow-specific lights to create others. While it is theater, and there is an abstract quality to the design of *Newsies*, what is great about Tobin's set is that it is tangible—there is something real. Although you don't look at those towers and say they are buildings, they feel like city structures. They feel like New York City. So the lighting tries to reinforce that.

There aren't many colors in the light that you wouldn't find in nature in New York. Whereas a lot of Broadway shows have a wide range of fantastic colors all over the stage, *Newsies* is not that show. And that was a choice. (Medda's scenes do push toward the colorful, but there would have been colored light in her theater in 1899.) After listening to the music, reading the script, and going through the set, my first questions to Jeff were, "Is the lighting approach like a rock show? How kinetic is it?" (Some shows have frequent and noticeable lighting changes and really look like rock shows on Broadway.) My sense for *Newsies* was that it was not that at all. It was Jeff's sense as well—"It is sort of like an old musical approach with an edgy feel to it"—which was great, because that is what I like to do.

Lighting research photo

Dressing for the Times

Newsboys, Gastonia, NC (Lewis Hine)

Jess Goldstein

costume designer

I had heard of *Newsies* but had never seen the film until I was asked to interview for the show. Since there wasn't a script ready for me, being a wise, old costume designer, I thought I should at least check out the movie. So I bought a copy of the DVD and knew within ten minutes that *Newsies* would be great onstage. It's like an *Annie* for boys. I was thrilled to have a chance to do it. The musicals that I've had success with, like *Jersey Boys*, tend to be a little more real. They're not the "lady in the red dress who comes down the staircase" kind of shows, not the big-sequined kind of musicals. And maybe that's how I get to do them—from my reputation doing plays and period pieces. Besides, historical periods are more interesting for a costume designer because, for one thing, you know more about the clothes than the actor or the director does, and your opinion is trusted more easily. In a modern show, everybody wears modern clothes, so everybody has an opinion on what is right for a character. With a period show, you bring a little more expertise.

Once I got the *Newsies* job, the research was pretty easy for me. I've worked a long time, so I have a lot of images saved in my studio, and I never have to go very far for this period. It's set in 1899, which is after the boom of photography, so it's very easy to find images of actual newsboys from this period. I was even able to find a wonderful photo of this man standing outside what looks like a house of detention with a group of boys. He was in a black suit, so that became the inspiration for Snyder—the perfect piece of research! The trickiest part was probably the vaudeville scenes with Medda Larkin. Women's vaudeville costumes of the period seem extremely old-fashioned and overly upholstered and heavy, so we had to find a way to lighten it up and make it more pleasing to the modern eye. We made them more colorful.

I thought it was interesting that Tom Schumacher strongly encouraged Tobin Ost not to design a quaint, old-fashioned set. They wanted something very modern and industrial. But to balance that, everyone understood that the costumes needed to be more "real." So there's a very nice juxtaposition onstage between the costumes and the set and projections. Also, Tobin didn't want to use any sepia tones—no browns. Everything should be steel and iron. And I tried to do that with the clothes. All of the poor characters are in blues and grays rather than browns.

Sketch of Brooklyn newsies by Jess Goldstein

ABOVE: Alex Wong, Tommy Bracco, Thayne Jasperson. FOLLOWING SPREAD: Additional costume sketches by Jess Goldstein

In order to make the fabrics realistic and believable, they had to be what the kids would have worn. But the knickers and the trousers are made of wools that don't have any stretch in them. So they had to be constructed in a way that could allow the actors to do these amazing splits and somersaults. It seemed a little tricky at first, but then we realized that these boys' bodies at that age are so flexible that they can make anything work. And we found that if they wore their waistbands way up on their waists, which is appropriate to the period, and get the crotch up very high, it allows them to do everything they need to. Some of them asked for a little strip of Lycra or elastic in the seam; it's only a half of an inch, so you can't even see it. It just gives the clothes a little stretch where they need it, but most of them don't even have that. And the clothes are loose enough where the padding needs to be, whether it's a knee pad or hip pad. We gradually negotiated with each dancer to see what was needed as the choreography developed. It was a very easy process. It's interesting that some of the boys, like the ones who are teenagers or in their early 20s, are a lot more flexible than the ones who are in their late 20s. That's just the age where the body really starts changing.

But the boys love the clothes. I wasn't sure if they would mind wearing their pants up so high, which is not what modern kids do now. But they all got into the clothes for the first time, looked into the mirror, and would say things like, "I would dress like this now if I could." They loved the texture of the clothes and the colors, and of course the newsboy caps, which seem to be coming back into vogue for guys. That was a happy coincidence. Since that look is very flattering to younger guys, it wasn't a hard thing to put over at all.

Landing the Job of My Dreams

Christopher Gattelli

I started dancing when I was eight years old. *Newsies* came out when I was finishing high school. Being so inspired by the movie, I had to make a decision. Am I going to college and take that route . . . or try performing? It had to be right around that time because I told my parents, "Give me a year to try it. Give me a year to get my feet wet in New York and see if I have the potential." Even at that age I knew that a dancer's lifespan is shorter than most jobs, so I figured, "Let me strike now while I'm still young enough and the iron's hot." So in that year I worked hard and I got my first job in New York City—performing in the Radio City Christmas Spectacular. I was only 17 and had to get working permits, etc. I was kind of like the boys in our show. I was still in school, but I did the Christmas show and then their Easter show that same year. That snowball kind of kept rolling and I ended up staying in New York.

Fast-forward to 1997, when I was performing a bunch and doing *Cats* in New York. The Gypsy of the Year competition that Broadway Cares runs was happening, and one of the cast members said, "Chris, you've choreographed stuff before. You should do something for our show." And I did a number for *Cats*. Tom Viola, the head of Broadway Cares, and Michael Graziano, their choreographer, saw it and said, "We'd love for you to choreograph the opening number of our Easter Bonnet event next season." I was like, "Oh my God!" Coincidentally, this was the year that the New Amsterdam Theatre was renovated, and we brought back five original Ziegfeld Follies women to be in the number. One of them at 94 still tap-danced, so we had the group tap-dance with her. Rosie O'Donnell happened to be sitting in the audience and wanted it for her show. So we did part of the number on *The Rosie O'Donnell Show*, which was in its heyday at the time. Soon thereafter, Jerry Mitchell, who was her current resident choreographer, had to take a leave from her show to do *The Full Monty*. Rosie said, "Well, what about that kid who did the number with the Ziegfeld girls?" I had done nothing, really, but I went in to audition and ended up being the resident choreographer for *The Rosie O'Donnell Show*! So I was doing double-duty between performing in *Cats*, then *Fosse*, and choreographing. After I choreographed *Bat Boy* Off-Broadway, my first real New York show, I decided to take some time off from performing. I still auditioned and performed a little bit after that, because I did still love it, but mostly I just started choreographing. I was about 25 at this point.

Fast-forward to 2011, when my associate Lou Castro and I were working on *Women on the Verge of a Nervous Break-*

ARTS & ENTERTAINMENT

CULTURE CITY | By Pia Catton

The Jump That Saved a Season

New Edition | Rarified Air on Broadway

At first glance, it might look like your garden-variety backup-dancer move.

RIGHT: *The Wall Street Journal*, April 30, 2012

down. Lou was the one who first brought *Newsies* up: "There are rumblings that *Newsies* is happening for the stage"—and I flipped! Fate is a very tricky thing, but I believe in it. My route to *Newsies* was a bit surreal. Lou and I talked about it and were completely jazzed about it, but nothing was confirmed at that point. Then I happened to be at an industry reading and ran into Jane Abramson, who produced a show I choreographed for the Fringe Festival in 2005. She said that she was now working in development at Disney and mentioned, "something, something, *Newsies* . . ." and I was like, "WAIT! It's really happening? I'm doing that show." She asked, "Would you want to?" and I just repeated flat-out, "I'm doing that show." I told her how much I loved it and how inspiring the movie was to me as a young dancer. She said she would get in touch with her boss, Steve Fickinger. By intermission, Jane came back and said, "Steve really wants to meet with you." I said that I would turn down anything to do this job. It wasn't even a question. I knew I had to do it. So I met with Steve and the rest is history. It was truly one of those things. I kept thinking, if I hadn't met Jane at that reading, would all of this have happened? I don't think my name was even in the hat for consideration at that point. I had never done a big dance show before. I'd done *South Pacific* and *Sunday in the Park with George*, which are more "musical staging" shows, so I don't think people knew much about me as a true choreographer yet.

Dance Auditions from Both Sides of the Table

Aaron Albano & Christopher Gattelli

AARON: I was beyond excited in 2010 to hear that readings of a *Newsies* stage musical were kicking around. I was doing *Mary Poppins* at the time and I tried every which way to get into those readings. Sadly, it didn't happen. But then it was announced at Paper Mill, so I (as well as the entire Broadway community) tried to get an appointment. When they announced that they weren't doing appointments, all of us showed up at the Equity Chorus Call auditions. *Newsies* was the first open call I can remember where even veterans humbled themselves for the chance to do the show they had grown up with. Reading the list of names was amazing—all the Broadway shows had their representatives. The wait-time of 20 years since the movie premiere got anticipation to a boiling point. Friends of mine from *Wicked* were ready to throw their production contract aside and say, "Let's go to Millburn." All of us were jumping to do it. I feel like a lot of Broadway gypsies wouldn't mention it in public, but it's the first time where it seemed you needed to pick the childhood dream over career. People were there who had done principal contracts before, or a thousand Broadway shows, but it didn't matter. We were all willing to take whatever we could get because *Newsies* meant so much to us. We got the chance to be a part of a phenomenon that we grew up with in such an influential way. It's not like we're going to get to be a part of the Teenage Mutant Ninja Turtles. This movie gave us the drive to do what we're doing now. It inspired us to become Broadway singers, actors, and dancers. And here it's coming back into our lives. Damn straight we're going to go for broke and try to get in it any way we can! Even if it's only for two months.

CHRISTOPHER: Even thinking about the auditions for the Paper Mill production makes me so emotional. Since this was my first big dance show, seeing these boys come in at their ages and doing what they were doing is hard to describe. I had no idea the talent was out there to that extent. Over a thousand people auditioned. A thousand people don't even audition for Broadway shows! They came from all over the country just to audition because they were such fans of the film. We had two rooms going at the same time because there were so many people. Lou was teaching a combination in one room and I was cleaning it up in the next. We just had to get through so many guys. They kept coming in and were so talented! It was completely inspiring to me.

AARON: My initial audition was for Chris Gattelli, Lou Castro, and Justin Huff. At the Equity Chorus Call, they were seeing a million people, which was still a small amount compared to the real open call. It was a small room and a lot of dancers all trying to kill it. Jaded gypsies try to pretend like they're too cool, like, "I don't need this job if I don't want it." This is the first time that none of that energy was there. Everyone was in it to win it. Like *A Chorus Line* in real life. Lou taught the combination, which is one of the favorite combinations that I've ever done.

CHRISTOPHER: I told Steve that I see the show as *Billy Elliot* times 20. These boys—this is how they communicate. Their motivation and their drive are through their physicality. They're youths—they should constantly be in the air and they should have fight. They need to keep rising to make their way to the big table. And I felt that technique is creatively important. Even though they're scrappy newsboys, their work ethic is so strong and they love what they do. Technically, these guys should be phenomenal because they care that much about what they do. For the audition, I put in a double tour. (One of my dance teachers growing up always said that for a male dancer, a double tour is like a female opera singer hitting a high C. Not too many people can do it. It requires complete control over all of your technical elements, strength, and prowess.) So I put one in the combination because I can tell a lot from that. And all these boys kept coming in and they were doing it. And they brought so much more to the table. Not only were they great technically, but they were smart actors within the combination. And then they sang! My head was exploding with joy. I will never forget that week.

AARON: The final callback day is the craziest audition I've ever been to. I will never be in a room of that caliber of dancers ever again. The talent of those 30 or 40 people was nuts. They were the titans of the dance world. You could see it in their work, and you knew the reputation of everyone there. And then you saw them dance like you've never seen them perform on a Broadway stage. The passion, the hunger, and the drive that we were all dancing with was unreal. The creative team said they could have cast the show three times over. And that caliber of dancer knows when they're doing good choreography. Everyone knew it and how to tell the story that Chris wanted us to. He had us do a portion of "Seize the Day." We danced the combination twice, first time as written, and then the second time we could add in tricks or gimmicks, staying within the realm of the choreography. It was a hard combination so it was rough to do it twice, but Chris could then see the type of dancer we were. Could we follow what he needed, but also what did we have to offer? He used both of those to cast the best show possible.

Garett Hawe, Kyle Coffman, Alex Wong, Thayne Jasperson

From the Alamo to the Big Apple

Andy Richardson

Romeo, Crutchie

In 2011, I was 16 years old and finishing my sophomore year in high school at the North East School of the Arts in San Antonio, Texas. My biggest worries were studying for the next English test and starting to scope out colleges. Now, those worries have evolved into trying to work my college schedule around my rehearsal and show schedule and "Oh jeez, I hear the subway coming. Time to run like the wind." I never thought I would be where I am today: living in New York, performing eight times a week in a show that I can't imagine my life without.

Originally, the audition notice for the Paper Mill Playhouse run of *Newsies* was for men ages 18 and up. When it was lowered to 16, I rushed to ask my agent for an audition. I flew up to New York, and after an initial audition of reading sides and singing a snippet of song, I got a callback to dance. In a tiny studio, with other guys ranging from their mid-teens to mid-30s, I learned a combo to "Seize the Day." I danced with all of the energy I could muster. I was called back to dance again the same day. After doing the same combo with a different group of guys, we were all asked to do a vocal workshop where we sang more songs from the show together. After that, I flew back home. Literally, as soon as I landed, I got a call that I was invited to the final callback. I must have looked crazy bouncing up and down in my seat.

In a gigantic studio with towering ceilings and enough room for an orchestra, I did my final callback. It was one of the most intimidating experiences I've ever faced. Most of the other guys auditioning were Broadway veterans who were years older than me. I felt like the runt of the litter. Not only that, but lining the front of the room was the entire creative team and production team: Jeff Calhoun, Christopher Gattelli, Harvey Fierstein, Alan Menken, Jack Feldman, and even the head of Disney Theatrical, Thomas Schumacher. It felt like Mickey Mouse was judging me silently from behind a table. That was when I truly felt like the underdog. Being surrounded by that mass of guys with sheer talent was daunting. When it was my turn to dance for the Mouse in my group of three, I took a deep breath and felt the music. I gave it everything I had. I danced. I read sides. I sang. I did flips. I even terrified everyone in the audition room by walking backward on my hands in a bridge like *The Exorcist*. (Hey, they remembered me.)

Tommy Bracco, Andy Richardson, Brendon Stimson

After it all, I flew back home and went back to school hoping for the call that would bring good news. I was in my sophomore English class, finishing a test, when I felt my phone start buzzing nonstop. Either it was broken, or I was getting a lot of text messages. Being the wonderful student I am, I slyly checked my phone under the desk. I see texts from my mom saying, "YOU GOT NEWSIES!!!!!!!" and I almost screamed in class. Since we weren't allowed to talk and my teacher was strict, I feverishly wrote a sign on a piece of notebook paper that said "I GOT NEWSIES" and showed it to my friends in class. Needless to say, we all freaked out and my English teacher got angry. It was so worth it.

Music to Move To

Mark Hummel
dance arranger

Christopher Gattelli has been my friend for 20 years. We've always wanted to work together, but he's never had a dance arranger. So he called and said, "I think I have a project that we can finally work together on." "What?" "*Newsies*." "Great!" "Jeff Calhoun's directing." I've known Jeff for 35 years and have written dance music for him. "Well, that's a no-brainer. Let's do it!" But I didn't know *Newsies* at all. Chris said it was a flop film in '92 and I thought "Oh yeah, now I vaguely remember something." I wrote the dance music for *Guys and Dolls* in 1992, which was huge for me. It starred Faith Prince and Nathan Lane and was directed by Jerry Zaks. So I was kind of busy with that when the film came and went. But Christopher, who is 15 years younger than I, grew up with this movie and always says it's why he's in show business.

We had pre-production and Chris said, "I don't know how this works. What do I do?" It is different with every choreographer, and I work with a lot of choreographers. My personal preference is that the music comes first. And he said, "Well, yeah." And I thought, "Okay, good. We're on the same page. But don't you want to tell a story through dance?" And he said, "That's exactly what I want to do." So I said, "So . . . tell me the story." And he did. I just took notes while he told the story of "Seize the Day" and "King of New York." Then I said, "Okay, let's go back. You said this . . . Thinking broad strokes, is that eight eights of music?" And he said "Oh, I didn't think about that. Yes." So I went on. "You have a transition there. Do you want that to be two eights?" "Yeah, probably." So that's how both numbers were created. I went home and wrote it, then came back and played it for him, and he cried. I said, "That's a good cry, right?" "Yes, that's a good cry, Mark." And then he got up and started to dance.

The broad strokes of the big dances settled in pretty quickly. And it was joy. Chris is lovely because he'd just tape it and say, "Go away. I don't need you to sit there and play the piano over and over." And he'd work things out with his associate to a recording. Then he'd call me back and say, "Basically we're okay, but right there I need something, here something more, etc." So we'd make some tweaks. Chris was choreographing "King of New York" when we had that earthquake in August 2011. Everybody went to lunch and read about it on the Internet. I was writing all through lunch, so when they came back and told me, I said, "Who would know? You all were tapping." We didn't feel a damn thing.

Besides being there for Chris, I was there in service of Alan Menken, whom I've known since 1983. We did a show called *Kicks* that never went anywhere, but most people know "I Wanna Be a Rockette" from that score. To make dance arrangements part of a score, you need to always return to the source material to support the dance music arrangement so it's one unit, one piece. I

Ryan Steele, Aaron Albano, Ryan Breslin, Jess LeProtto

learned a big lesson from Marvin Hamlisch when I did *The Goodbye Girl* with Martin Short and Bernadette Peters. He saw a big production number choreographed by Graciela Daniele and invited me and the orchestrator Billy Byers over to his house after rehearsal. He said, "Now, what's this right here? Where's my melody?" I said, "Ohhh." He said, "You could put my melody right here. Don't lose anything you've written, but my melody could go over the top of your dance music in longer melodic lines." It was a wonderful lesson, because that's what makes a good score—when it's all combined. So since then I figure out what's needed for choreography and then what sounds goods to weave back in the score—which is what composers like, because they know that they will be well served. I'm always in the style of the composer even if I'm not playing his exact tune the whole time (because that's just dull!).

Andy Richardson

Discovery, Rigor, and Rehearsal

Aaron Albano

Getting the casting call was pretty great—a childhood dream come true. Then I had to tell *Wicked* that I needed to leave to go do this regional show at Paper Mill. On the playground growing up, before I even knew what I was doing, I would sing "Santa Fe." And one of my first audition songs was "King of New York." I just had to do *Newsies*.

Thom Gates

production stage manager

I was working with Jeff Calhoun at San Diego's Old Globe on a musical production of *Emma* when he told me he was going to be working on a stage adaptation of *Newsies*. You could see the excitement in his eyes. Near the end of our run, Jeff asked me if I would be interested in being part of the production, and I was. Just prior to rehearsals, the designers, Jeff, Ricky Hinds, and I got together at Tobin's apartment to go through how the show would move with a model. It was quite powerful to witness how everyone in the room worked together to create the free-flowing show we have today.

Lou Castro

I moved to New York when I was 18. I was always asking people, "Have you seen *Newsies*? Are they bringing it to Broadway? Where can I audition?" Years passed, and I started working with Christopher Gattelli as an associate choreographer. I always knew he was a perfect fit for the show. So when he called to say, "I just got the offer to do *Newsies*, and you know what that means . . ." I screamed out loud . . . and bawled inside!

Ben Fankhauser

I graduated from Ithaca College in May 2011 and auditioned for *Newsies* in June, over only two days. The first day I went in and sang "Seize the Day" and did some of the scenes. I got a call to come back and dance that evening. Right afterward I got a call for a final callback the next morning. An hour after my final audition, my agents called me to say I got the part! The audition process is rarely that short, so looking back, it seems it was meant to be!

Aaron Albano

Truth be told—and I think a lot of Fansies will attest to this—I would watch *Newsies* up until "King of New York" and then fast-forward to "Once and For All," because everything in between was the boring stuff. Before I started on the show, I just kept thinking, what's going to happen after "King of New York"? All the fun numbers are done until the end! When I read the script for the first time, I thought, "Wait—why does Brooklyn come in all the way at the end of act two? They should be there for the fight! And why is Jack an artist? Why is there this? Why is there that?" But something Harvey Fierstein told us in the first few days has really stuck with me. He said that the difference between writing for film or TV and writing for theater is that writing for film is story-driven; writing for theater is theme-driven. The challenge in transferring *Newsies* from screen to stage was that you had a story, but you couldn't tell what the show was about. A couple of boys getting mad doesn't make a show. A show about a revolution is different. When all the events became focused on that theme, *Newsies* started to take off.

Ben Fankhauser

At the first day of rehearsals, we did a table read and Alan Menken sang all of the songs that were new to the show. At the end of act one, Jeremy Jordan sang "Santa Fe." It was (obviously) incredible. Everyone stood up and applauded. I thought, "This is going to be something major. And this guy is the vehicle driving the show." I was amazed by his ability to sing so perfectly, sitting down, at 10 a.m.

Thom Gates

The first time I heard all of our boys sing in a vocal rehearsal, I knew this show was going to be special. The sheer force behind their vocals with that raw male energy was something you don't witness every day. When we started to put those vocals together with the dance numbers, that excitement level could be felt

Aaron Albano, Jess LeProtto

throughout the entire rehearsal studio, tearing through everyone involved, from the production assistants to the artistic staff. We knew we had something special.

Christopher Gattelli

When we started choreographing, we came up with a set of vocabulary to describe how guys would dance down the street. We named these groupings of choreography in "Carrying the Banner"—things like "Kick the Curb" or "Hopscotch." How would we dance on a curb? Then we would come up with the physicality to match it. In "Carrying the Banner," I tried to keep it street-like. It's full of flexed feet and rougher around the edges, but still strong. By "Seize the Day," my idea stylistically is that they become this army, this unified group. You see these boys grow into men before your eyes. Their lines become stronger, their feet point. Everything becomes a little more grown up and specific. It's something that the audience might not be aware of, but we know it's under the surface.

Aaron Albano

Chris wanted none of us to be dancing the same thing until "Seize the Day." Ever. There is some unison movement, but it's angry, explosive, unstructured, and unfocused. We have individual expressions of energy on our own. It's not refined. We're just separate guys until "Seize the Day," when we become the army, the union. The first thing we do out of the gate is the double tour. It's the first time that the audience sees us as a unit. When Chris told us that story, I got chills.

Christopher Gattelli

The first time I saw those boys do "Seize the Day" in the rehearsal room, I knew. I'll never forget it. You could see it in their faces, in the faces of the creative team. You could just tell that something magical was happening with this show, with the group, everything.

Mark Hummel

My first sense of the potential impact of our work came at the beginning of rehearsals, when there was reaction in the middle of dance numbers. Everyone in the room applauded, and that was terribly rewarding, because we weren't going for that. To get the reaction in the middle of the number, you stop and say, "Gosh, I guess we're doing something right."

Danny Troob

My job on *Newsies* was to be very different now, 20 years later. I was doing orchestrations only. I was never at rehearsal, which was foreshortened anyway, because of Hurricane Irene. I met no one I didn't already know. Almost nobody knew I had worked on the movie, including Jeff Calhoun, our director. And it didn't matter. Since this was intended for licensing, I had only 12 musicians to work with (three of whose parts had to be "detachable"—i.e., add-ons) and very little time to orchestrate the entire project. But I got it done!

Christopher Gattelli

Since so many of our cast members were very young, it took a lot of trust to shepherd them through the process. I tried to make them feel as comfortable as I could, because I wanted them to leave their mark on the show, to have their DNA in the show forever. Twenty years ago, I was them. Twenty years ago, I would have been dying to do this show. To have the opportunity when you're that age, working as hard as you do and practicing your technique and your tricks to make yourself stand out—I know what that's like, and I did not take it for granted for a second. I wanted to honor their talent and time and work ethic.

Ben Fankhauser

The second day of rehearsal we were dancing, and I brought my jazz shoes like an idiot. I had no idea what I was doing. Chris taught the combination in five minutes and everyone had it. I was like, "Wait! What? Slow down!" Then we spent the rest of the morning doing what he calls "The Circus McGurkus." One by one, everyone had a chance to show what tricks he could do. It was insane. People were doing backflips off tables, off chairs, to the left, to the right. We were putting together "King of New York," and Chris asked if anyone was comfortable doing a bunch of pirouettes. Like six in a row. I thought there might be one show-off who would be able to do it. And then everyone raised his hand. You keep thinking that not all of these guys could be this good. Not everyone can do everything. But they all can. It's surreal. I didn't think that existed. How could one producer find all of those people for one cast? So one of the first passes of "King of New York" ended with all these guys doing six pirouettes.

Bryan Bradford

production assistant, stage manager sub

"Towers moving!" was a battle cry for the production assistants hired specifically to move the three rehearsal towers. Most Broadway musicals will have about two production assistants on the stage management team during rehearsals. For *Newsies*, we had six. In the rehearsal room at New 42nd Street Studios, the iconic towers were only one-and-a-half stories tall to fit the height of the studio and were made of wood. And they were heavy! It took two people to move each tower on cue, which was as choreographed as the dances themselves. Running a number multiple times would require the towers to be reset to their original positions each time, and would begin with one of us yelling, "Towers moving!" as a warning to anyone standing on or near them. Needless to say, after running a number like "Carrying the Banner" several times a day, going to the gym wasn't necessary.

Christopher Gattelli

Most shows are a combination of careful planning and happy accidents. We came up with the "newspaper dance" in the room during preproduction. By the end of the day, there were newspapers covering the studio—*The New York Times*, *am New York*, different versions, different sizes—we went through so many trying to figure it out. We intended this to be

Rehearsing "Seize the Day"

the boys stomping on Pulitzer's *World* and their livelihood, making a mess of it, literally shredding it into the ground. But when we got to the end of the dance, we had no idea how to get rid of the papers. Then when we got to rehearsals, I think it was Evan Kasprzak who jumped off them, did the donkey kick (the handstand thingy), and picked up the papers on the way up. I never would have thought that was possible. And this is how they were the entire process—the guys all said, "Oh, my God—that's so cool!" (Well, Tommy Bracco said, "That's wicked cool!") And all of a sudden, they were throwing themselves on the floor until they could do it. Even Jeremy Jordan. He's got to sing "Santa Fe" in a minute and he was still diving in. Once they had them, we were like, "Well, let's just throw them into the house. We'll figure it out." And they loved the idea. So that turned into our props department creating our own 1899 version of a newspaper. I love that they get to do it for storytelling purposes, but since it goes out in the audience, people get to see that it wasn't a trick, that they didn't use anything special like some slippery material. And that they see it's an actual 1899 newspaper. We have reams backstage since we go through them so quickly. Now it's an iconic moment, and it was just thrilling to be a part of creating that.

Bob Tzudiker

Tom Schumacher, a friend for many years, assured us that *Newsies* would see the stage. Eventually, he made good on his word. This New York tale had returned to its home turf in the oldest medium: live theater. We came from California as often as possible to experience the making of *Newsies* for the stage, and the cast's energy and enthusiasm was a blessing to us.

Bryan Bradford

One of my main duties during the rehearsal process was to maintain the master script, which meant receiving daily changes from Harvey. I remember receiving up to 30 pages of changes on some days. I was so impressed by how "not-precious," for lack of a better phrase, he was with his work—fearless about cutting things that he knew weren't working and open to playing with something new. Jeff Calhoun set an amazing tone for the production from the very first rehearsal. He was calm and kind, and that spirit spread through the cast and crew and continues even as new people are brought into the production. It really makes it feel like a family, and going to work feels less like work and more like hanging out with good friends.

Ben Fankhauser

Newsies is such a beloved story. It seemed like everyone had such a close connection to it that no one had any doubt it was going to be good. Everyone trusted each other. Since we didn't have any pressure to make sure our show had a life beyond Paper Mill, we were able to focus on the work and the best way to tell the story. We were super excited, and it was such a blast making this show.

Jeff Croiter

When I first read *Newsies*, I thought it was pretty great. And then I sat in on some rehearsal. I'd pop in for 10 minutes here, 15 minutes there, and everything I saw was inspiring. First of all, everyone in the room (cast, directors, choreographers)—the whole team—was a joy to be around and so welcoming. I always made a point of stopping by because I enjoyed it there. When I saw a full run-through in the rehearsal room, it blew me away. For a show that didn't even have any tech elements yet—it was just people dancing around the room and singing on rehearsal scenery—I thought it was spectacular.

Lou Castro

The rehearsal process was tough and rigorous. I give all credit to my dance teacher, Gary. He was so hard on me, but he made it fun. That's how we did preproduction, built the dance music, and ran rehearsals. But we had an incredibly talented cast who loved each other, loved the movie, and loved telling this story. You can feel the connection and bond onstage and backstage.

Christopher Gattelli

The rehearsal process for this show was much smoother than most, and I credit that to Jeff. I have never worked with anyone more trusting. He was so gracious and collaborative. And because Jeff was a choreographer, there was an innate sense of trust and freedom. I would propose ideas and he would just say, "Go! Just run with it." Then he'd give feedback: "Maybe we should do that step two times longer because it'll stick in their eye more," or, "Maybe that section is a little too long." He was a phenomenal editor of my work . . . and so fantastic to work with. I don't remember anything about it being hard. It was all joy.

The Fight of the Century

J. Allen Suddeth

fight director

First came a phone call from Paper Mill Playhouse. Then, "Do you want to fight direct *Newsies*?" Me, "Sure. What is it?" I must admit, I had never seen the movie, nor had I heard of the project, but I was happy to work for Paper Mill, and, as it turned out, for Disney Theatrical too. But it was mutual—Disney had never heard of me, either. So began my journey of creating one of the biggest fights on Broadway in decades, in the year that I turned 60.

I first chose all the fight props: a padded barrel for Les to hide in safely and for Jack Kelly to throw at the Delancey brothers; various baseball bats and batons for the Goons to fight with; "stunt" (lightweight) newspaper bundles to throw; asking set designer Tobin Ost to create a removable "cart slat" for Davey to fight Wiesel with; padding on the set (the cart floor and the balcony near the ladder) for actor safety; and padding for the actors (a full set of professional-grade baseball catcher's gear is worn by the Delancey brothers to protect them from full-contact strikes by the crutch on the leg and chest).

Then I went to work creating the fights. I spent about four hours roughing out the brawl the first time, much to the delight of director Jeff Calhoun, and then continued to refine and detail each actor's track. There are leaps, falls, punches, contact kicks, a bite, a couple of strangles, an elbow strike, and multiple changes of fight partners. I trained the cast how to safely perform these techniques, and we rehearsed it multiple times.

Once on set, the task became more difficult, as many of the fights entail running up into the towers, and fighting 20 or even 30 feet in the air! Finally, to archive the choreography, it took three assistants and me weeks to notate the moves. It is permanently set in stone now in a huge Excel document with each move, change of partners, blocking change, and entrance detailed and color-coded for 20 actors.

The cast rehearsing the fight on stage in its entirety before the performance

Ben Fankhauser, Andy Richardson, Ephraim Sykes

Passionate Foot Forward

Eduardo Castro

When it was announced that we were going to do the pilot production of *Newsies*, I just knew I had to be a part of it. There was no question in my mind that that project was going to be part of my time at Disney Theatrical. In 2011, I was overseeing pilot productions of *Aladdin* and *Newsies*—very loosely, because both were regional productions aimed at testing the content and potential of shows that Disney was developing. I had been helping out as a production liaison with *Aladdin* at the 5th Avenue Theatre in Seattle during the spring of 2011, but when Anne Quart arrived to take the productions reins, I came back to New York and I started focusing on *Newsies*. I sat in that game-changing meeting for Tobin's revised set, with the towers—how great that was!—and started to meet the creative team and the Paper Mill staff. I didn't know yet what my role would be, but I threw myself in wholeheartedly.

When rehearsals started, I went across the street to New 42nd every day. Sometimes I would just sit there for a number, sometimes I would be there for a couple of hours, sometimes I was there the whole day. Just to be present. And to learn: to see how Jeff worked, to see Chris work, to just get a sense of what the show was—every detail. Once we began run-throughs, I really just felt part of the team. I remember coming back to the office and giving Tom little updates, here and there, about how things were going or just overall feelings about the show. I just knew that somehow, it was the right time for *Newsies*.

Nick Scandalios from the Nederlander Organization came to a final studio run-through at New 42nd and sat in front through all of act one. At intermission he had to leave, but he pulled Tom aside for a brief conversation. After the run-through, Tom, David Scott (licensing manager), and I came back to the office. I remember Tom was by his exercise machine and I was being my crazy self: "This is so good. It's gotta be going to Broadway!" And Tom said, "Well, you know, Nick just basically offered us a theater." And I was like, "Come on! What are we waiting for?"

Tom, of course, is very smart and said, "Look, there are a lot of things that you connect to in a room, because first of all you are five feet from the actor who is screaming or crying or laughing. There is that visceral reaction because you are right there. But then as soon as you move that to the main stage, and depending on how the big set actually ends up looking in the house, the energy can dissipate." I kept that at the back of my mind when we got to Paper Mill for tech. I was still so excited at rehearsals, and I would come back from Millburn and talk to the creative department every night. They were just as excited and were so good about keeping my fire going.

Anne was mounting *The Lion King* in Madrid, so I was present as the Disney production liaison in case something was needed, which empowered me to feel like, "Okay, I can definitely make things happen." Maybe it was a naïve way of looking at things, because what power did I really have? Not a lot. But it was fun to at least be there and keep on learning about the show and working with the creative team, which for me was incredibly valuable—to sit at the table next to Jeff Croiter and see his lighting patterns develop, or talk to Sven about how he decides what projections he wants to put where, or have Jeff Calhoun ask, "What do you think of this? Does it feel right?" And for me not to be afraid to say yes or no.

And that little crack in the door of interest from the Nederlanders was in the back of my mind. When you have that carrot dangling in front of you, you are going to run until you get it. I knew that if we delivered at Paper Mill, then there was a chance of not just getting to that crack in the door, but actually pulling the door open and just pushing all the way through. I wanted to get this show to be seen, to Broadway, to get it to success.

And it wasn't just about the show. Seeing the cast's excitement and commitment, the creative team's designs and ideas and choreography and direction . . . for me it became a fight for them. I didn't want that experience to end. I didn't want it to be just four weeks in rehearsal and four weeks in New Jersey. I wanted that to go on. And I wanted to see how amazing and long the journey could be.

The Real Test Arrives: The Audience

Nick Sullivan, Mark Aldrich, Laurie Veldheer, John Dossett

John Dossett

Pulitzer

When you've been doing this as long as I have—34 years as a professional actor in NYC—you try to limit your expectations. I've had shows close after five weeks on Broadway, a six-month pre-Broadway tour that didn't last six weeks, and one show close before it ever opened. So I came to *Newsies* with the simple thought of having fun for a few weeks and being able to drive home between shows, see my wife and son, and have dinner. And then rehearsals started. I wasn't called in for rehearsal that much initially. My part is rather insular from the newsies. So it wasn't until I watched the initial first-act run-through, and saw for the first time the spectacular level of artistry and talent involved in the production, that I had an inkling I was part of something very special. This was confirmed by the through-the-roof audience response at our first preview at Paper Mill—a response that only grew as the run there progressed, amazing us all, as we stood in the wings watching its special alchemy unfold.

Jeff Croiter

When we moved into the theater, the people who were working with me on the lighting team—some from Paper Mill, some Broadway people—really got into the show. And that's how I know if something is really good. If the people on the crew, who ultimately see way more shows than most people, think it is better than most things they have worked on, then I know there is something special about it. They really loved it. Over a dinner break, I walked up to the programmer, and he was humming one of the songs from the show. So I was like, "All right, this is good!" And I loved watching the audience watch *Newsies*. People were nuts for it from the very beginning.

Chris Montan

I was probably like everybody else—it wasn't until previews at Paper Mill that I knew we had something more. Well, maybe you could feel it during our sitzprobe—it really popped that day! And you kind of went, "Hey, this thing has a lot going on, and unless I'm crazy, people won't even remember what didn't work about it!" But I never dreamed it would go beyond Paper Mill and the licensing ambition at that point. I certainly could never have projected Broadway. People did a lot of things right, naturally. The first day I saw the set . . . it just was such a great idea. They gave it all that dynamic energy. People could appear anywhere, at any height—on a roof, in a tenement, in an office. It was really, really smart. And it sure didn't hurt to have a guy like Jeremy, who could be masculine in the part and still sing a lot of numbers. It was like the old John Raitt days, where these really handsome guys enter and bang out these songs with self-confidence. Jeremy helped galvanize the whole cast around a strong, masculine Jack Kelly to set the tone for the show.

Bob Tzudiker

The production was intended as a trial run for licensing, but no one knew the size or passion of the Fansies. Social media played a huge role in getting the word out. We are not avid Facebook users, but it was irresistible to track the tens of thousands of people who were following the *Newsies* page and the hundreds who were making their way to Millburn from all over the country. Their cheers as the opening bars were played at Paper Mill had an incredible, visceral power.

Emily Powell

In 2004, I got hired by Disney Theatrical to work in production. Shortly after starting, I inquired as to why *Newsies* had never been done onstage. Elusive "rights issues" was the consistent answer. Since I clearly didn't understand "rights" at the time, I vowed with my coworker Matt Cronin that if Disney wouldn't make a *Newsies* musical, we would, no matter what it took! And every chance I got, I made certain everyone at DTG knew that if the show were to make it to Broadway, I had to work on it. Fast-forward to 2011. After leaving DTG for four years, I had returned to work on the national tour of *Mary Poppins* and found out that Disney was collaborating with Paper Mill to put *Newsies* onstage. I figured this might be the one and only time it would be produced professionally, and I couldn't miss it. So I booked a flight from Chicago to New Jersey for a 24-hour trip to see the show. Although I of course noticed that some lyrics were different from the ones I knew so well, it was a magical experience to see the show finally come to life.

Danny Troob

We opened at Paper Mill and were not "dead on arrival," to quote Jeffrey Katzenberg's description of the movie opening. We were warmly greeted by critics and audiences alike. Our story was right in sync with the Occupy Wall Street movement. And where did all these Fansies come from? I had not, you see, been aware that *Newsies* had had a second life on the Internet and had a group of very loving fans who could hardly wait for the show to open. And the vibe among professionals in New York was very positive. People I hadn't heard from in a while started calling to congratulate me on the show. And I started hearing from people I didn't know at all, but who knew my work, and were looking for an orchestrator. Of course, many years had passed—I was now in my early 60s. Some of the original film newsies came to previews, and they were now the age I had been when we worked on the movie. I wasn't ready for that. But I was ready for a streak of good luck, which our successful opening ushered in, and which seems, knock wood, to be continuing . . .

Mark Hoebee

The real key for me was putting the show in front of our subscribers, whose median age is 62. Most of those people had no idea even what *Newsies* was. At our first Thursday matinee, which is our heavily subscribed senior audience, I thought, "This is going to be a test." When they stood up at the end and loved it, it was a real eye-opener, a huge turning point in the potential of this musical. And throughout the run, patrons reacted viscerally and emotionally to the show. I think one of the reasons *Newsies* is so powerful is that it's almost entirely men. It has a different energy than a show with a mixed or female-dominated company—a testosterone-built engine that drives it

Kara Lindsay, Jeremy Jordan

in a different way, and the audience reacts to that, whether or not they are aware of it.

Eduardo Castro

I would go into David Schrader's office right before heading out to Paper Mill and just ask him straight out, "What has to happen to take this to New York?" He would throw back a litany of questions about audience, sales, marketing, percentages, budget, etc. But it was more validation for my crusade—like, okay, now I have to answer those questions if I want to convince him. And those lyrics and lines from the show were constantly in my head—they just kept me going and kept me pushing. One time he said to me, "Eduardo, you don't even know what the reviews are going to be like." That is when the *Times* review came out. And I did the whole bit in his office where I came running in with *The New York Times* review, which happened to be above the fold. And I was like, "What else? What else do you need to make it happen?" It was part of my crazy obsession.

Alan Menken

We mounted the show at Paper Mill and then . . . "Watch What Happens"! "The World Will Know"! "Once and For All"! People come. People cheer. Critics rave. Theater owners descend. We "Seize the Day"!! It's improbable, but true. And I feel like the "King of New York"!!!

"A musical worth singing about! Even for the cynics among us, *Newsies* has a stirring, old-school sincerity that's hard to resist."

—DAVID ROONEY,
The New York Times,
September 27, 2011

Dreams Fulfilled

Noni White

Apparently, I wasn't the only one dreaming all those years of *Newsies* onstage. Almost every original cast member of the musical has told us they do what they do (dance, sing, act) because of *Newsies*. One of the many things I love about the stage show's choreography is that Christopher asked these boys to do things with their bodies that seem almost impossible, and yet they've made it balletic, athletic, poetic, acrobatic, militaristic, and very modern without ever taking you out of the period. And as all great choreography does, it advances the story.

Director Jeff Calhoun has a similar temperament to Kenny Ortega and runs his stage like Kenny ran his film set. He's open and collaborative, supportive and demanding. He creates an atmosphere of trust and gets great work out of his cast and crew. I've always said to our son, Ben, "Some of the best teachers I've had in my life were tough—not mean, but tough." Both Kenny and Jeff are incredibly warm, generous, embracing, and exacting directors.

I have to admit that I really didn't like the character of Katherine at first. Sometimes it's difficult to let go of things you love in a story, and Bob and I loved the girl newsie Charlie as Jack's love interest. We felt that Katherine took it from a David and Goliath story to a David and Goliath and Goliath story. We wanted it to be the kids' victory. I first began warming to Katherine because of my fondness for Kara Lindsay in the role. Kara is such a wonderful human being. She's smart and funny and gifted and quite modest. Jack Feldman's brilliant lyrics for her new song, "Watch What Happens," and Alan Menken's great music closed the deal for me. Katherine is someone who would go on to be a suffragette, which makes me very happy. I have now fallen in love with Katherine, plain and simple.

When we opened at Paper Mill, I knew that our beloved *Newsies* would finally have its day in the sun. The show was still not considered Broadway-bound, but the audience response to previews and opening night was spectacular, as were the reviews. I have never been in a theater and experienced that kind of energy before the curtain went up. The excitement in the room was palpable; the buzz in the theater went straight to my heart. The audience reaction was an affirmation of what I had always envisioned.

Later in the run, Paper Mill hosted a "Fansie Night," when a number of devoted fans came to see their beloved movie turned into a play. Bob didn't go with me, but I wouldn't have missed it. Kenny and some of our original movie cast members also came that night and joined in a Q&A session with the audience. Part of my fully embracing *Newsies* onstage was seeing it again and again, enjoying the audience enjoying the show. I saw a young woman in the ladies' lounge who was loaded with merchandise she had purchased in the lobby. She was there with her mother and saying how much she enjoyed the show. She then asked if I had anything thing to do with *Newsies*. When I told her my husband and I had written the screenplay, she burst into tears! Then her mother began to cry! They told me how much the film meant to them, how it had shaped the young woman's life and the lives of many of her friends. She kept saying "You have no idea what that film meant to me and my generation."

Hope Dancy & Friend, Glen Ridge, NJ

Jonah Robinson, Sherman Oaks, CA

Alexa Reyes, East Brunswick, NJ

Jessica Gleason, White Plains, NY

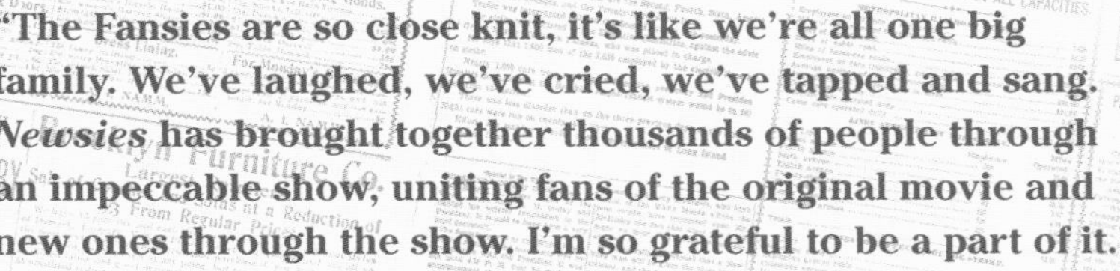

"The Fansies are so close knit, it's like we're all one big family. We've laughed, we've cried, we've tapped and sang. *Newsies* has brought together thousands of people through an impeccable show, uniting fans of the original movie and new ones through the show. I'm so grateful to be a part of it."

— Alexa Reyes, East Brunswick, NJ

Melanie Cleveland, Orangeville, Canad

"I will never forget how inspiring *Newsies* was. There was an entire ensemble of male dancers who were all incredible. I had been dancing for four years and I came home from my trip to New York and had this fire and motivation to continue to pursue dance and musical theater. *Newsies* really changed my life. It showed me specifically what I was working toward."

— John Tupy, Tulsa, OK

Parker Austin Green, East Brunswick, NJ

"It gave me a chance to remember when my sons were little. This was one of the first musicals they saw in the movies and it helped give them an appreciation for the genre. They watched the video over and over and sang and danced along. This show is very special to me. When I saw it, I couldn't help but be transported to a very happy time."

— Roberta Hartman,
Tonawanda, NY

Liz Hornbach, Philadelphia, PA

Erika Panzarino, Somers, NY

"Ever since my best friend and I watched the movie in fifth grade, we have been obsessed. We wanted *Newsies* to become a play so bad and even spent days planning out the trip to New York we would take if it ever came to pass."

— Erin Matthews, Tiverton, RI

Carly Palmatier, Zeeland. MI

"In 1992, I saw the movie in theaters and loved it. Jack Kelly was my hero. For the next ten years, it was my main fandom, before I knew what fandom was. I made a website, I wrote novelizations, I bought press kits and stills, I bid on memorabilia from Christian Bale, I wrote fanfic. Finally by 2002, I felt I'd gotten too old and out of touch to stay involved. I took down newsies.org and newsies-movie.com and retired. For the next decade I grew up, or tried to. Then I found out about the Paper Mill production. I tried to be circumspect about it, but this was the dream. I flew to New York in April of 2012 to watch that dream come true."

— Jmar Gambol, Manila, Philippines

FANSIES

Christine Mantineo, Saddle Brook, NJ

FANSIES

Clara Kennedy, Wausau, WI

"It's proven to me that everything is possible, no matter who you are, what kind of life you lead, or how tough the odds may seem. The choreography makes my heart stop."

— Rachel Silverstein, Media, PA

Hannah Stengele, Toms River, NJ

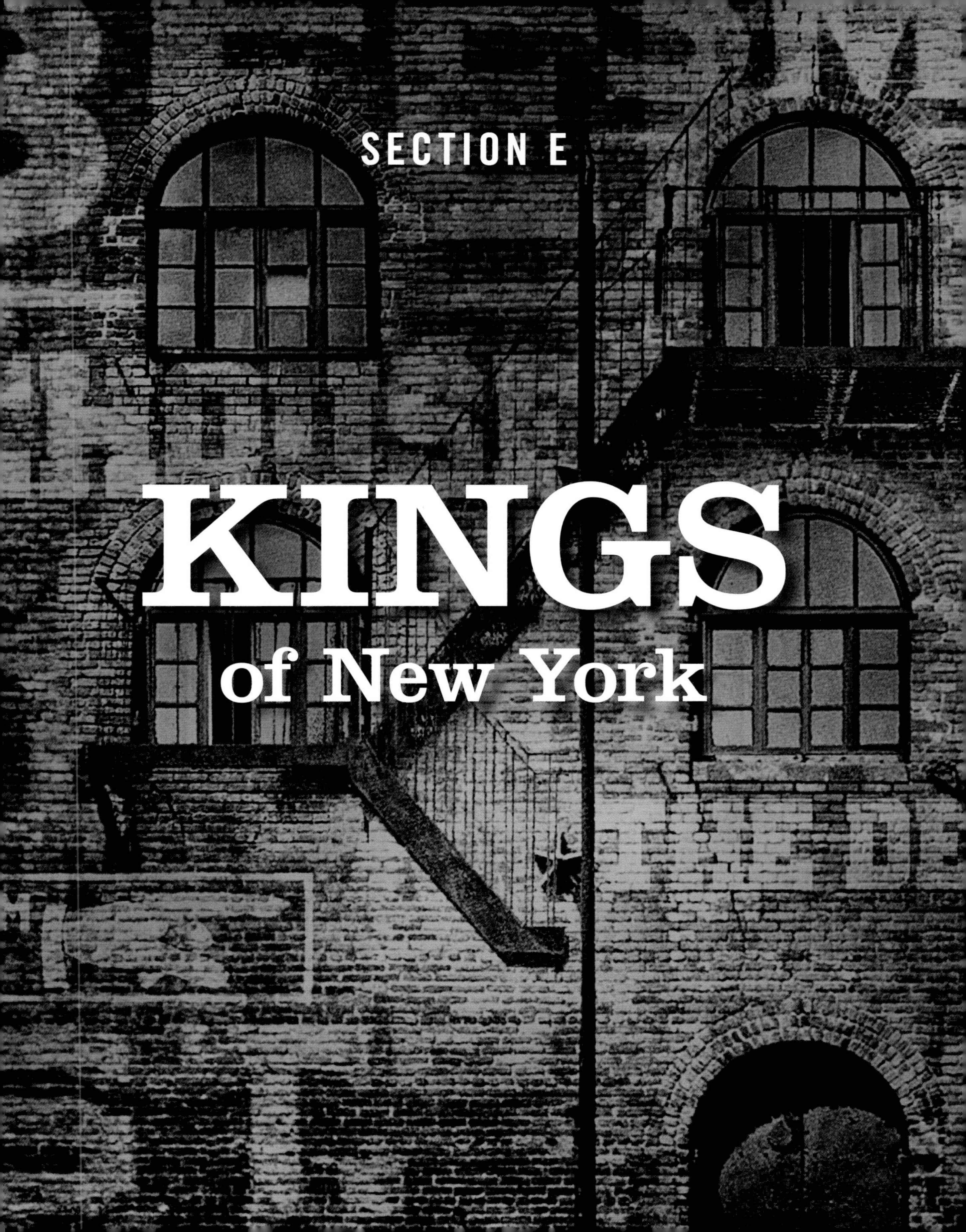

SECTION E

KINGS of New York

"Extra! Extra! *Newsies* Coming to Broadway"

Andrew Keenan-Bolger
Crutchie

When I decided to write about my favorite *Newsies* moment, I had trouble choosing just one. There's of course the first day we moved into the Nederlander—jumping up stairs two at a time, scouting the dressing rooms, and then stepping onto a Broadway stage, many of us for the first time. Certainly opening night was memorable—fighting back tears as 1,200 people simultaneously leapt to their feet following "Seize the Day." The Tony Awards, *Good Morning America*, jet-setting to L.A. for 24 hours to perform on *Dancing with the Stars*; all of these memories were unforgettable, but the one that hangs most vividly in my memory didn't occur in front of a cheering audience or on a television screen. My favorite *Newsies* moment came on a chilly night in November, the day we learned our show was moving to Broadway.

People never believe me when I say our cast was just as surprised as the rest of the world to hear of our transfer. Of course, there were rumors floating around the dressing room, but I refused to let myself get comfortable with the idea. On the evening of November 15th, I remember heading to work at *Mary Poppins* (the job I returned to after our regional run at Paper Mill). In the time it had taken me to get on the subway, grab a smoothie, and walk to my theater, the news had broken. As I pushed through the stage door, our associate director greeted me wielding his smart phone: "Extra! Extra! *Newsies* Heading to Broadway," he read off his screen. I'm pretty sure I dropped my smoothie.

The press release led to a text explosion among the boys, likely causing permanent damage to whatever satellite happened to be hovering over Midtown that night. After the performance, Garett Hawe (fellow *Newsies* and *Poppins* cast member) and I practically skipped down Ninth Avenue to meet up with some boys from our cast to celebrate. Sliding into a booth on Restaurant Row, I remember telling our waitress that she'd be seeing a lot more of us. "Our show is coming to Broadway!" I shouted. She nodded politely and slowly backed her way into the kitchen.

We began fantasizing out loud. "Oh my God, I hope we get to perform on the Tony Awards," Ryan Steele grinned. "I'm totally going to deck out our dressing room," said Ben Fankhauser. "I hope we get to do a fashion spread in some fancy magazine," Garett beamed. "Newsboy chic is so in this season!" "OMG merch!" Ryan Breslin cried. "They should totally make us *Newsies* trading cards."

We crawled our way through Midtown, toasting the dream life awaiting us in the new year. As we pushed our way into some dive-y spot on 45th Street, a man grabbed me by the sleeve. "Um, excuse me, are you guys the newsies?" he squinted. It was the first time we had ever been recognized. "AHHHH!" we screamed. "Yes, we ARE the newsies!" We crammed our bodies into a dusty photo booth, taking a series of goofy pictures. It felt unlikely we'd ever forget this moment, but just in case, it might be smart to have a hard copy.

Our evening took a dip when I got a call from Jeremy Jordan. He sang us his congratulations and explained how happy he was, but I could tell there was heartbreak in his voice. He was scheduled to star in *Bonnie & Clyde* that month, now unable to lead our production. We assured Jeremy that he'd have a ton of fun in his new job and promised not to like any "Jack" more than him.

I don't remember whose idea it was to head over to the Nederlander Theatre, but as soon as it was uttered, we slammed down some crumpled bills and jetted back into the winter cold. Ryan Breslin, overcome with excitement, dove into a massive pile of garbage bags lining the curb. "EW! Bres, get out of there!" Jack Scott squealed. "Why?! We're going to Broadway!" he said, brushing coffee grinds off his jacket. "Yeah, but that's just disgusting."

As we rounded the corner on 41st, we must have looked like a scene from an actual Disney movie. The vacant 3 a.m. streets became a concrete runway. We burst into phrases of Chris Gattelli's choreography, hopscotching and jeté-ing toward the awning where our marquee would soon hang. We took pictures, belted out songs, and scooped up gutter snow from the previous week's blizzard, packing numb fingered snowballs and pelting them at the Nederlander's front of house. "Wait, why are we throwing snow at our theater?" Garett finally interjected. None of us had a good response, so we began hurling them at each other, laughing through chattering teeth.

I guess it seems strange that my favorite memory of doing a show didn't involve any actual doing. My time spent with *Newsies* was a blast, and each moment seemed to top the previous, but the thing I loved the most was just getting to be there. I left the show a little more than a year after that day in November. To be honest, it still feels weird not walking through the stage door every night, seeing the faces of my cast mates, more brothers than friends at this point. Sometimes when I'm running errands in Midtown I catch myself hanging a detour, passing the theater where all these memories were crafted. I remember how I felt gazing up at the Nederlander Theatre that night, picturing what the walls would look like with our faces plastered on them, praying that the world would love the show at least half as much as we did, and realizing that the guys standing next to me were probably gonna be my best friends for the rest of my life.

Managing Necessary Insanity—Together

Anne Quart &
Geoffrey Quart
technical supervisor

ANNE: Everybody has his or her own moment. Nick Scandalios had come to a rehearsal run-through in the studio and said, "This is great! Where do you want to go? To the Nederlander Theatre?" We all responded, "This is for licensing!" My moment came during opening night of Paper Mill, when I felt for the first time that *Newsies* was something more people deserved to see. But it wasn't until later that Nick actually made the Nederlander available. And then it became a conversation about the cost of moving to Broadway. If we were going to play only 12 weeks, which is what we all believed there was a market for, then we couldn't spend millions and millions of dollars to load it in and market it. The great news is that in order to make it available to other licensees, we had built the set to move, so we'd go in pretty quickly. Geoff had been with Troika Entertainment for seven years, moving shows that close on a Sunday and open on a Tuesday, so he knew better than anyone how to get a show in fast.

GEOFFREY: There was some discussion of tour options at some point during Paper Mill, and I came in to look at what the tour could be, from a technical perspective. Within a couple of weeks, talk quickly turned into moving *Newsies* to Broadway, and then I was sort of the guy who knew more about the show than anyone, even though I had spent maybe three days at Paper Mill tech.

ANNE: I knew in my gut, and Tom I think as well, that unless we had someone who wasn't going to come in with preconceived, rigid notions of, "It takes six days of pre-rig, plus three weeks of load-in, plus two weeks of dry tech...," it would not work because it would simply cost too much. And frankly, the show didn't need all that. We needed a super-aggressive schedule, and we needed somebody who would make it happen. Geoff has never loaded in a show in any other way, so he believed it in his soul that this is what happens, that this is what we were going to do. Not to say that there wasn't agita at the kitchen table over a bottle of wine . . . I had been working on *The Lion King* and *Mary Poppins* for years, but *Newsies* was the first Broadway show that I was opening from the ground up, and it was Geoff's first Broadway show, period. We'd come home at the end of a day and be like, "Okay, so sound thinks they need three more days, and lighting thinks they need three more days . . . and all those days add up to three more weeks. We can't do that, so what can we do?"

GEOFFREY: When you work on a show with your wife . . . we actually got to a point at home where we had to say, "Okay, we have like an hour, and that is when we are going to stop talking about the show," because there was a lot going on with all the different departments that had to be serviced on every level. We had to figure out how to get our cast a good eight-hour session dedicated to playing with the towers, which were so integral, almost dancers themselves in the show. After Paper Mill, we set up the show in the shop again and reprogrammed all the video-screen automation so that once we hit the stage with the boys, no one was worried about that. We didn't want the creative process to be bogged down by the technical process. We wanted to be ready so that changes could come easier if Jeff saw something he wanted to do. There was a point where we were going back and forth about how many weeks in the rehearsal hall versus how many weeks onstage. We must have run 15 to 20 different schedules with the same budget to see how it all fit, to come up with the best plan. It was all about providing a safe and professional platform to allow the creative team all the openness and ability to play that they wanted.

ANNE: But everybody knew the load-in schedule was still supertight and superrisky. I remember the first production meeting, and many people said, "This is crazy. This is a crazy amount of time. It's never going to happen." We just kept pushing, "It's what it's gotta be." And to his credit, Geoff took a stand with an established system and said, "We're gonna figure this out."

GEOFFREY: I spent so much time in the truck doing shows on the road, with shortened production schedules, that when someone comes to you and says we need to do it in this time, you don't go, "Well, that is impossible." You go, "Okay, well, that is crazy, but how do we do it?" So we figure it out. We needed to load it in in a week, have a week and a half with the cast onstage, and then begin previews. So you set about figuring out how to do it, putting the right sort of people in production places. I have Sam Mahan, who worked with me at Troika for the longest time. We don't waste time questioning how we're going to do it—we just make a great plan up front and then never fear to change it. Because if you are so rigid with your plan, then something gets in the way and you can't see past it and you never get it done. I just keep going around to each department and finding out where they are and what they need and how they need it done and what I need to do to get out of the way so they can finish task A so that task B, C, and D can be done behind it. It is a bit of negotiation—well, 14 hours a day of negotiating. On the road, you have a big wing space to spread out, but in the Nederlander we were on top of each other from day one, and on certain days I was probably guilty of bringing far too much stuff into the theater than was actually possible to deal with on that day. Because we did it all onstage, we had to account for how to get the stuff off and out of the way as quickly as possible.

Projection console during technical rehearsals

ANNE: The crew at the Nederlander leapt with us, because they could have brought it all to a dead screaming halt. They could have just said, "There is no way that any Broadway show is going to load-in in a week. We are going to take the three damn weeks that we are used to." But they didn't. I think they jumped because they wanted a hit. They wanted Disney in there. They wanted something that was going to run. Geoff did a great job of saying, "We're all in this together, and we have to go!" When we got in the building, we felt like we were on the same page and we loaded in the damn thing in just over a week! The big twist of load-in, of course, was that Geoff and I found out we were having a baby. We had not expected that additional level of complication. It was well past our opening that we publicly told people, so we were on a secret journey for a while. I remember standing at the back of the house during load-in and showing Geoff the first ultrasound, "We are going to do this show, and we are going to have a baby."

GEOFFREY: When we came out of that production meeting, there were a lot of doubts about tech. Then in the first couple of days, where we got to where we sort of wanted to be, everyone was getting on the same page. They all jumped in and did it, whether or not they thought they could. There is also a certain level of, "On the 14th we are bringing an audience into this building no matter what." We did have a tight budget, so it wasn't like we could just start throwing people at it like it was some sort of rock show. Not only did we do it in terms of the timeline, but we also, for the most part, did it mostly within budget. And we had the right group of guys, including Phil Lojo on sound and electricians Jim Maloney and Brad Robertson. We all said, "This is the craziest, stupidest thing we may have ever done, but we're here, so we might as well just do it."

ANNE: I remember making a decision in the second week, when they wanted to work through the day off and it was going to cost another $40,000, that we just couldn't do it. There had to be another way. (And I couldn't drink through tech, which was also very tricky!) It was a constant ballet of who took priority each day. Because of the tight and unprecedented schedule, the fact that Geoff and I had a shorthand helped expedite it. We'd come in the morning with a clear idea of how we were going to get each day done. We did a week and a half in the theater, we had the cast onstage for just over a week, and then we were in front of an audience! It was our first Broadway show, and we were expecting a second child. It was a lot going on at the same time. We didn't know if we could do this, but we took a leap, together. Here we are a year later and we have this beautiful show and we have a beautiful little girl. So for us, personally, it was a huge journey. Through all this, I'm most satisfied with the fact that I didn't let the fear get to me. There was a lot to be afraid of: we weren't going to be able do it, we weren't going to be able to deliver monetarily... there was a lot at risk. I promised something to Tom and David that I actually didn't know if I could deliver. There was not a day that went by that I was not terrified. But I didn't let the fear get to me. Geoff and I were in it together. And the show benefited from that connection.

The Brick (or, Slipping on an Old Pair of Shoes)

Jeremy Jordan
Jack Kelly

Newsies was one of my favorite movies growing up. I tore through that VHS tape so hard that my mom ended up having to buy multiple replacements. Jack Kelly was my idol (followed by Aladdin, then Simba, and of course, all of the Mighty Ducks). Jack might as well have been the older brother I never had. In fact, I'm pretty sure that even as a kid growing up in South Texas, I had mastered the "New Yawk" accent by the time I was 10. I had newsie running in my blood.

Fast-forward 16 years, and there was Jack Kelly once again staring back at me, but this time from sheets of paper: *Newsies: The Musical*. Just a bunch of words and lyrics thrown together, but I saw him clear as day. In our premiere production at Paper Mill, playing Jack was like slipping on an old pair of shoes: comfortable, familiar, and full of dirt and grit. I loved every second of it.

Unfortunately, all those seconds only added up to about two months and a few days. And just like that, our time in Jersey was done. On the eve of our final performance, it was uncertain what the future held for *Newsies*. Were we going to tour? Go straight to Broadway? Or was this gonna be just another rabble-rousing flop like the movie? No one knew. However, one thing was certain. Whatever the fate of *Newsies*, this was going to be my final bow as Jack Kelly.

Another show I was involved in, *Bonnie & Clyde*, had announced it was coming to Broadway before I had even begun rehearsals for *Newsies*. The dates had been set, and about two weeks before the run at Paper Mill was over, I was rehearsing *Bonnie & Clyde* in NYC during the day and performing *Newsies* in Jersey at night. What a crazy couple of weeks that was! I even got a pretty cool article in *The New York Times* written about the whole ordeal. It was all incredibly surreal and exhausting.

But even amid all the chaos, my 10-year-old self never seemed to lose sight of the fact that though Broadway stardom was awaiting me, it meant having to say good-bye to Jack Kelly. For good. Because I knew *Clyde* was going to be my ticket in. My first starring role in a new Broadway musical and man, it was a juicy one! Sex, guns, bank robbery, love, death—this was gonna be the smash hit of the season! I mean, Jack Kelly was a cool guy and all, but he didn't get to shoot people and seduce a chick while playing a ukulele naked in a bathtub! I was trading in my newsie cap for a pistol, my rooftop for an open road, and Santa Fe for the slums of West Dallas. Life was moving on, and it was moving quick.

I didn't see it coming, the overwhelming sadness, until I was standing on the makeshift rooftop during that final Paper Mill performance, Crutchie at my side, an audience below, and this lyric on my tongue: "Soon your friends are more like family, and they're beggin' you to stay." After that, I was done for.

Kara Lindsay, Jeremy Jordan

Every word I spoke in that evening's show was like a brick, heavy with meaning and falling upon me with a pain I instantly recognized as longing. Longing for one more chance to perform this show, to again be the leader I had proven I could be and guide it on its path to an inevitably grand future. Longing for some miracle of fate that would lace me back into those beautifully familiar shoes.

But *Newsies* closed, and the next day I was Clyde and Clyde alone. It was odd at first, but my New *Yawk* quickly took a trip down south to an easy drawl. And pretty soon, life was great again. It truly was. And then, during previews it was announced that *Newsies* would be headed to Broadway in April. The brick fell again. "This is it," I said to myself, "the day has come when I have to sit back and watch Jack Kelly come to Broadway without me." I could taste the bitter more than the sweet, but I was going to have to accept the fact that my journey with *Newsies* had truly ended.

Well, then *Bonnie & Clyde* opened and it was the best night of my life. True Broadway greatness was on the horizon. But the next morning, the reviews came out, and suddenly greatness didn't quite feel like the right word. Over the next month, we struggled, campaigned, and fought with a fervor and grit that any newsie would be proud of, but after just 69 performances, we were through. Soon it was just another casualty in the war of Broadway—like its title characters, young and hopeful and ripped apart.

I found myself once again saying goodbye, speaking lines and singing lyrics with an utterly earnest finality. But as my lovely costar, Laura Osnes, and I reached the last moments of the show, I realized something felt different this time. The brick was gone. The lights began to fade, I closed my eyes, and there before me stood my old friend Jack Kelly once again, smiling. And waiting. I opened my eyes and the show was ending. Bonnie and Clyde were exiting forever in an ear-splitting fury of gunshots . . . but to me, the sound suddenly became something different altogether. It was the sound of heavy rain on a New York City rooftop. It was the sound of tap shoes clanging down a metal fire escape. It was the sound of an old printing press bursting to life and declaring in big, bold letters, "JACK IS BACK!!!"

Broadway Dreams in Sight

Eduardo Castro

I knew I was the crazy man in the office with this obsession for *Newsies* and bringing it to Broadway. Our financial analysts would try to sober me up by giving me projection spreadsheets and saying, "Look, with an unknown title you are going to sell maybe 60, 65, and if you're lucky, 70% of the gross potential. And it is a small house, so the upside is slim at best." I know their job is to point out risks, but they seemed so nervous. They just didn't see what I saw. I got to the point where I had to look at their projections and say, "This is wrong; this is wrong; this is wrong. It is going to be at 100% every week!" I just had to say it that way. Yes, we had an unknown title for the general public, but the show was amazing, and it was only a matter of time for that news to spread. In my mind, *Newsies* was going to be successful no matter what. There has to be at least one crazy person to push for the long shot, and I guess it was me. When we finally got the green light, the transfer ended up happening so fast, and there wasn't any real *Newsies*-dedicated staff yet. I said, "That show is not going to move without me." There was no way that anybody was going to tell me otherwise.

Stuart Zagnit

Swing

This creative team is a remarkable group of really competent, experienced, focused people. I've known Harvey and Jeff for years, and I was the last Seymour in the original *Little Shop of Horrors*, so I've known Alan from the beginning of his career. As a newcomer to *Newsies* for Broadway, I could see during rehearsals that consideration was paid to everyone working on the show. And most of that attitude I credit to Jeff. He told us at one point: "You know, when I was a young chorus boy, I didn't think about the crew and the other people who worked at the theater. I didn't think it was important to say hello. But I've come to realize that a show is successful only when there is mutual respect for everyone." And this respect has become infectious. It has created a very comfortable atmosphere among the cast, crew, musicians, wardrobe and hair, and even the house staff and ushers. Between Paper Mill and the Broadway opening, every available moment was used and nothing was wasted. Everyone was committed to improving the show, and I think that's what made it a hit. I remember Harvey coming in with a rewrite of the first Pulitzer scene, and then Alan arrived and they introduced the new number, "The Bottom Line." Then Jack came in and began tweaking the lyrics, which totally blew me away. To watch him dissect the song, pull it apart, and then put it back together was really like a master class in musical theater. The lyrics in this show are just phenomenal.

Alex Wong

Sniper

Being a part of *Newsies* was like nothing I ever imagined. I always knew that I wanted to be on Broadway at some point in my career, but I would have never guessed that it would have happened at this moment. On the first day, it already felt so right. After the initial dance rehearsal with the amazing Christopher Gattelli, I walked into the musical rehearsal. We all took our places around the piano and I knew there was no other place I wanted to be. It was a quick learning curve for me, to be taught the show in just a few weeks, as nearly everybody else had been a part of the Paper Mill cast and I had actually never done a musical before. However, I would go home every day and review the material with a big smile on my face, so happy that this was really happening. Within a week, I already felt so comfortable with the guys. It seemed unreal that a cast could get along so well, but we weren't just a cast anymore, we were a new family.

Emily Powell

On Tuesday, November 15, 2011, the announcement came: *Newsies* would be moving to Broadway. Without a moment to spare, I e-mailed Anne Quart to inform her of my more-than-mild interest in the assistant company manager position. Five minutes later, I received the most amazing response I could have expected: "I am not going to torture you any longer than I need to. Eduardo is going to CM the limited run and we would love you to come to New York. Let's talk details in the next couple of days." And the rest, as they say, is history!

Ben Fankhauser

One of my favorite aspects of being in the show is getting to dance. I wasn't really trained in dance as a child, but I was always a good mover. I love to dance, although I don't have the technical versatility of the guys in our cast. As Davey I feel like, "Wow, I'm actually doing it. I'm one of the guys!" I definitely relate to that sometimes. When I'm dancing with some of Broadway's best, I can't believe I'm in this company. There's a section in "Seize the Day" that I didn't do at Paper Mill. Jeremy and I would run off to the side and let the professionals do their work. And any chance I had, I would go to the black box theater at Paper Mill and practice that combination over and over again. When we came to Broadway, I approached Chris and told him that I had been practicing it for months. He said, "Well, let me put you in and see how it looks." He put me in the back behind Alex Wong and I thought that was a great place for me to be. Doing "King of New York" and getting to tap dance is also a huge thrill for me. Like Davey, I'm thrilled to be in the gang and do what the guys are doing.

Tommy Bracco announcing the Broadway transfer live on television

Kara Lindsay

Katherine

I remember coming to the Nederlander Theatre for the very first time to tour our dressing rooms, backstage, etc., and begin tech. That's when it became real to me. Broadway was actually something tangible now rather than a thought or dream or hope. We all went out onto the fire escape up near the dressing rooms and screamed and laughed—we were so excited!

▲ Jeremy Jordan, Brendon Stimson, Jeff Calhoun, Thayne Jasperson

▲ Mark Stys, Timothy Eaker

▲ Thom Gates, Ricky Hinds

▲ Kara Lindsay

▼ Michael Fatica, Jack Scott, Caitlyn Caughell

▲ Lou Castro teaching "Carrying the Banner"

▲ Tobin Ost, Jeff Calhoun

▲ Thayne Jasperson ▼ Mike Faist

▲ Garett Hawe ▼ Ryan Steele, Alex Wong

▲ Andrew Keenan-Bolger, Jeremy Jordan

Tweaking for Transfer

Jess Goldstein

I knew from the first day of rehearsals for Paper Mill that *Newsies* was going to move to Broadway—no matter what anybody said! Just seeing all of the excitement in the room as the cast went through the music, it seemed like the timing was perfect for this show. We had such success with Paper Mill that most of the changes I made for Broadway were to make things out of a little more expensive fabrics. At Paper Mill, we bought the boots that became the tap boots in "King of New York." We just added the taps because we didn't have enough money to make a second set of custom boots. On Broadway, we needed to make sure they could last a long time, so everything was custom-made.

Jeff Croiter

The phone calls for Broadway started like, "Hey, we're thinking about maybe doing this. Come over to the theater and have a look." Then, "Hey we're a little closer." At a certain point, I had to say, "I'm booked. But of course, if you are telling me that *Newsies* is moving to Broadway, I will be un-booked." So finally—really late in the game for most Broadway shows—it got the green light. The idea was to do it as fast as possible. In fact, it was the fastest schedule for a Broadway musical that I have ever heard of. It's unbelievable how quickly it went. But we all knew what we wanted, and we did it.

Mike Faist, Ryan Breslin, Jeremy Jordan

Mark Hummel

I felt that the dances at Paper Mill were good. When Broadway was announced, everyone said, "Let's make 'em longer." So that's what we did. Dances for both "Seize the Day" and "King of New York" were elongated. Now there's the spoon section for "King of New York" and a longer statement of Menken's tune at the beginning of "Seize the Day"—two choruses instead of one (with a modulation, of course!). When Michael Kosarin offered me the Broadway conducting job, he said, "It's yours if you want it, but can I ask why you want it?" I said, "Because I love the piece and I'd like to conduct it eight times a week."

Jeff Croiter

In order to get *Newsies* up quickly, we had to take the lighting cue files from Paper Mill and load them into the computer in New York. We knew we wouldn't have time to start from scratch re-teching the whole show. Ideally, the lights would hang in the exact same places as at Paper Mill so that when we turned lights on, they would line up with what we had done. Onstage, everything from the proscenium back is pretty much the same light plot that we used at Paper Mill. But from the proscenium out into the audience was totally different. After the renovation, the Nederlander didn't have any lighting positions at all, so we had to manufacture pretty much everything from the ground up. Being a lighting designer is not without its pressures. During tech, you sit in the middle of the room, and everyone stares at you and waits for you. But it pays off in the end—whether it is the people or the experience or the audience appreciation. It's always nice when the audience likes the work you are doing!

Jess Goldstein

As much as I love research, sometimes you have to sacrifice historical accuracy for theatrical efficiency. At one of the very last previews, they wanted me to cut Katherine's hats. She wore one at the beginning of the show, and I kept thinking that it seemed so inappropriate for a young girl, or any person for that matter, to go without one. When you look at those newsreels of people walking down the street, everyone is wearing a hat, no matter how poor or rich they are. It was just part of the outfit. And because Katherine is a professional, it seemed to me that her arc is that of someone who takes herself very seriously. The hats seemed to be important, but I lost that battle. At the end of the day, it needs to be what is best for the show as a whole, which was pretty great.

Catching Up for a Big Broadway Sound

Ken Travis
sound designer

I had gotten to know the Disney staff while working on *Aladdin* at the 5th Avenue Theatre, so Anne Quart called me after *Newsies* was announced for New York. I think I was in college when the movie came out, so I had actually never seen it. I watched some B-roll from Paper Mill, but my first live experience of it was in rehearsal. And it was insane—because it was a really small room with low ceilings and two-story-high pieces of scenery that came rolling within a foot of us and guys doing fan kicks over our head. I was like, "What the hell?!?" It was amazingly thrilling.

The biggest challenge for me in the Nederlander was that Tobin and Jeff Croiter and everybody had already worked a lot of things out at Paper Mill. So I was playing catch-up and had to work within the confines of designs that had already been fully vetted and tested. When they said, "We need lights here," I'd be like, "Well, I need to put a speaker here." It was hard to come in and make an argument when I hadn't seen what they'd dealt with. Everyone was collaborative, but we learned more on the fly than I enjoy. A good example was "King of New York." We saw that in rehearsal and said, "Hey, there is a tap number in the show!" In other productions, we had built a special deck that we miked in a particular way. But they already had the deck from Paper Mill, so Tobin said we could hide some mics on the stage, and then we built wireless mics into the tables.

The towers didn't pose any sound problems other than the fact that they move and it is a much more three-dimensional set than usual—with three stories! At the end of a couple of numbers, when a tower is all the way downstage and the actors' heads are like two feet from the main speaker source for the whole show, we are always just clenching a little bit: "Man, they are so close to the speakers. How doesn't it feed back?!?" We had a few monitor issues with people hearing

Loading the deck onto the Nederlander Theatre stage

Members of the original Broadway orchestra: (back row, L-R) Ray Kilday, Steven Malone, Tom Murray, Mary Rowell, Mat Eisenstein; (front row, L-R) Ed Shea, Brian Koonin, Deborah Assael-Migliore, Mark Hummel, Mark Thrasher, Dan Levine, Paul Davis

and seeing things onstage because of the towers, but that was pretty easy for us to fix. Sound designers actually don't care about the set so much; we really care about the house, because that is who we're serving. So if we can get accurate measures of the house, it's just a lot of trigonometry. The sound of the show in this situation, where the set is big and open, is fairly simple. We are telling a simple story with a big, theatrical presentation. We are not hiding the fact that we are amplifying it, and we really get that house rocking a couple of times. I like it kind of big!

The weirdest place for sound in the Nederlander is, ironically, front-of-house, right where the mix position is. Kai Harada had done *Million Dollar Quartet* in there and warned me, "Don't stand at the mix console or you'll go crazy." We were a week into tech and I was getting so frustrated. Then I remembered what he said and moved out, relieved: "Oh, it sounds really good here!" A lot of these old theaters weren't designed for amplification, so there are boxes where we need to put speakers. The house was built to keep a warm sound all the way to the back, but now with these big sound systems, it ends up being a little too boomy in the back of the house, so then we have to kind of counter it as much as we can. Gabe Wood and Cassy Givens, our sound engineers, will periodically come out from behind the board and walk down to an aisle because there is just some weird anomaly that has to do with the shape of the house.

Unfortunately, they never get a break. *Newsies* is really hard to mix! But we try to build in once or twice a week where they come in and help the other one out to make sure the mixes are right, especially if you just put a new person into a role or if we thought we heard something weird. And then I come in once a month and audit the show and give them notes so we are all on the same page. I often sit at front of house or in the middle of the balcony—it is a great show from up there! Of course, we also have those amazing audience responses to factor in. The first time we did the show, we didn't even hear the trumpet. As soon as the lights dimmed, the audience was so loud that I thought that we hadn't turned the mics on! I went back to do a cleanup in the one-year anniversary week, and during two of those performances there were moments where the crowd was so loud, I just started laughing, "Yeah, we'll never beat that!"

Broadway Previews

Pam Young

director of creative development, DTG

I work out of Disney's Burbank offices but was lucky enough to be in New York and asked to attend the invited dress at the Nederlander Theatre on March 14, 2012. I wasn't sure what to expect. I was one of "those" who liked the movie okay—certainly not hugely impressed and definitely not a "Fansie." As a theater veteran, I don't usually erupt into tears during shows; I get teary, perhaps, but not running-down-your-face tears. At *Newsies*, I was hooked from the first moment. But what was extraordinary was the first choreographed number, "Carrying the Banner." The energy permeated throughout the house, and when the number was complete, the audience erupted into applause that lasted well over a minute. But that wasn't the best part. At least five of the dancers onstage erupted into tears, their hearts overflowing with joy. I can only imagine their Broadway dreams had been realized a hundredfold. Being a jaded critic of theater is easy; what is difficult is to be so utterly moved by actors onstage, loving what they are doing. I was invited into their world, became a part of it, and tears rolled down my face.

Christopher Gattelli

First preview on Broadway is hard to describe. To see that performance, knowing my history with the film and what it did for me, and then to sit in a Broadway theater knowing that I participated in helping bring it to the stage, and then to

hear the audience respond the way they did . . . I can't even put that into words. The Nederlander Theatre is so intimate; even from the back row you feel so close to the stage, and the cast feels that audience energy. When "Seize the Day" got a standing ovation, it blew my mind. I could never have imagined that I could ever contribute to something like that. But to then have it happen after "King of New York," all during the first week, it doesn't get any better than that.

Lou Castro

During the first preview I was sitting in the audience with Chris Gattelli on my right side, and Noni White and Bob Tzudiker on my left. Just before the performance was about to start, as the house lights were dimming, Chris grabbed my hand and said, "You are sitting next to the authors who changed your life." I started bawling! How do the stars align for something like this? It was the most amazing feeling to experience that incredible night with the people who I thank on my left and trust on my right.

Bob Tzudiker

The depth of audience passion for *Newsies* came home to me at the final preview before the Broadway opening. I was sitting next to a very young woman who had flown in from San Antonio, Texas, just to see the show. During the intermission she overheard that the couple sitting next to her had written the movie. Just before the lights came down for the second act, she grabbed my arm. "You have no idea how much this story means to my generation." And she spoke about the themes, the spirit of the story, its politics and power—exactly the things we care about. In that moment, all the hope and heartbreak, the hard work, and great good fortune collapsed into one gratifying moment. We take immeasurable pride in having helped to bring this story to life. The real newsies deserved nothing less.

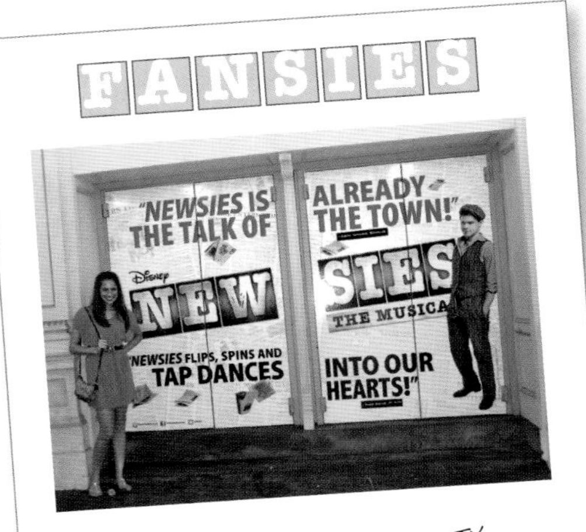

Wendi Reichstein, Houston, TX

ON FACEBOOK! *NEWSIES* ATTRACTS MORE THAN 100,000 FANS BEFORE BROADWAY OPENING.

EXTRA! NEWSIES NAMED A CRITIC'S PICK BY ENTERTAINMENT WEEKLY, USA TODAY, AND THE DAILY NEWS

"A barnstor

Red Carpet Arrivals:
Max Casella; Kenny Ortega;
Noni White, Benjamin Tzudiker,
and Bob Tzudiker; Jack Scott
and Michael Fatica

"A triumphant resurrection! A sentimental old-style Broadway chest-sweller of the first order."

– New York Magazine

"*Newsies* is an irresistible, high energy

ng, four-alarm delight!"

– *Time Out New York*

Robert Iger and Thomas Schumacher

Lewis Grosso and Matthew Schechter

Jack Feldman and Alan Menken

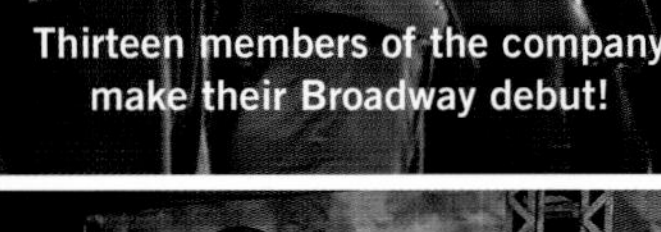

Thirteen members of the company make their Broadway debut!

Aaron Albano wears the Gypsy Robe, an honor given to the ensemble member with the most Broadway credits.

ON FACEBOOK! 2,000 PEOPLE POST ABOUT *NEWSIES* ON OPENING NIGHT

ner!" – *Entertainment Weekly*

The Tony Awards

The company riding the bus to the Beacon Theatre on June 10, 2012

On May 1, 2012, *Newsies* received eight Tony Award nominations: Best Musical, Best Performance by a Leading Actor in a Musical (Jeremy Jordan), Best Original Score (Alan Menken and Jack Feldman), Best Book of a Musical (Harvey Fierstein), Best Direction of a Musical (Jeff Calhoun), Best Choreography (Christopher Gattelli), Best Scenic Design of a Musical (Tobin Ost and Sven Ortel), and Best Orchestrations (Danny Troob).

At the awards ceremony at the Beacon Theatre on June 10, Alan, Jack, and Chris took home statues.

Alan Menken

Ah . . . the Tonys. I spent about 20 years pretending that the Tony Awards meant nothing to me, ever since *Beauty and the Beast* came up short in 1994 (although our musical went on to have a very healthy run of 13 years). The experience of *The Little Mermaid* was much the same. Ditto *Sister Act* and *Leap of Faith*. For some reason, when I was the new kid in Hollywood writing scores for Disney animated musicals, they couldn't throw awards at me fast enough. But back home on Broadway, it was tough to win the big award. And I was reconciled to that reality. Then came *Newsies*, in a year when I had three shows running simultaneously. And at the Tonys . . . they called my name! I acted calm. I acted cool. Backstage, journalists and colleagues all gushed and celebrated my "long overdue" Tony. I was happy and numb at the same time. And now my little silver Tony Award sits in the middle of all the Oscars and Grammys—front and center, where it belongs. And it does mean a lot.

Jack Feldman

No matter how you feel about awards in general, it's hard to imagine a young theater nerd with a heartbeat who hasn't fantasized about winning a Tony. It felt, and still feels, surreal, and winning it with Alan, a friend for 40 years, was a gift. A couple of hours later I got to the party that Disney hosted for us, and there in one large room were all the

Alan Menken, Jack Feldman

ON TWITTER!
28 MILLION PEOPLE REACHED BY MORE THAN 8,500 PEOPLE POSTING DURING THE 2012 TONY AWARDS!

people I'd spent so many months working with, getting to know and then to love. And suddenly they were engulfing me (my first-ever engulfment). I was physically and emotionally overwhelmed. For me, *Newsies* is, among other things, about the power of family—and define it any way you like—-to make us feel stronger and better than we ever thought we could be. Yes, the award was a dream come true, but no more so than my great good fortune to be a part of the loving and ever-growing family that is *Newsies*.

Christopher Gattelli

Opening on Broadway and then getting a Tony nomination was one amazing thing after another, but I tried my best not to get swept away. I had been nominated for *South Pacific* and I remember going on that ride. You're so overwhelmed and you never really expect to be nominated. The Tony Awards are something you grow up watching on your television so it has this feeling of being untouchable, almost other-worldly. You don't even think about it ever being a possibility. I remember going through the circuit in a daze because I couldn't believe I was at these luncheons sitting next to this caliber of people. Some of them had been my idols for years. With *Newsies*, since it was the second time around, I made sure I just enjoyed it. I enjoyed every moment because it's rare to even get a nomination. I had a really great time on this journey and I wanted to remember every moment. This show is so special to me and it meant so much to be there.

TOP: The cast watches backstage as Christopher Gattelli accepts his Tony.
ABOVE: Christopher Gattelli

Making the Deals for Mass Appeal

Jeremy Jordan, John Dossett

Seth Stuhl
director, business and legal affairs, DTG

It's 1992. *Newsies* completely missed me the first time around. It came and went when I was in the middle of college, and musicals about dancing kids weren't on my friends' radar, even my theater friends. We were far too sophisticated (i.e., stuck-up) for that. Although we weren't too old for *Beauty and the Beast*, which had already been anointed by Frank Rich as the season's best musical and had a fancy showing at the New York Film Festival—that was the Disney musical for 20-year-old sophisticates. By the time *Newsies* was out of the movie theaters (quickly), all I knew was that it was a flop and it had Ann-Margret, which I thought was kind of cool (go see the film version of *Tommy* if you don't understand why).

Cut to 2004. Through my own bit of serendipity and incredible luck, I end up leaving a big fancy law firm to work as a lawyer for Disney Theatrical. I tell colleagues and friends. All I hear is *The Lion King*, *Beauty and the Beast*, some more *The Lion King*, and then, a few whispers in the dark—okay, maybe a few over-excited shrieks, demands, and pleas—"*Newsies* . . . when is it coming to Broadway?!?" All from friends 25 years old or younger, before belting out a few notes of "Santa Fe." There definitely was an age line-in-the-sand here, between the clueless older generations (myself included, dare I say by the skin of my teeth) and the beyond-enthusiastic younger ones. Over the years there is the occasional rumble in the halls about developing *Newsies* into something. I'm a lawyer, so I keep my mouth shut to my friends. No way I'll be the source of any leaks!

Cut to 2011. *Newsies* is really happening. And it is happening enough that I can finally tell some of my younger friends, who do a few pirouettes of joy—their dream was coming true. But it was still simply for licensing, and then a nice, simple production at Paper Mill Playhouse. We all know what happened then.

Cut to October. I've been fortunate to work on a bunch of Broadway shows in my time at Disney, but I've never seen anything like what happened from when it was decided that *Newsies* was going to cross state lines to dance onto Broadway. As production counsel I felt as frenetic as the newsies leaping from tower to tower and spin to spin—there were agents to banter with, deals to do, contracts to draft, images to clear, logistics to work out. The job for a lawyer to a Broadway show is to clear away all that business stuff, worry about the details, and draft all the fine print so that the creative folks—the people who make the magic—can get their job done.

You know when Jack Kelly spits in his hand and says, "It's a compromise we can all live with," before shaking hands with Pulitzer? That's what I do every day, making deals we can all live with. Usually it takes years to get a show on Broadway. Here, the process was condensed into five months—five months!—and the spit was flying all over the place. Confession about theater lawyers: we all love theater. And we all love a big-kicking, big-singing musical. And we all love every theater cliché, the comeback being the best of them all. And ultimately, *Newsies* is a show that every lawyer should love. Isn't Jack Kelly just another lawyer, making deals, negotiating with his clients (the other newsies) and his adversary, Pulitzer, making compromises everyone can live with, even if he's a hell of a lot cuter than the rest of us and can hit an A?

So while I had never worked more frantically on a show, I also had never worked with and "against" other lawyers and agents (we all kind of like each other, hence the quotes) in such an environment of loving the show we were negotiating about, and loving the journey that the show was on. We were all pushing that little engine up the steep hill, together. I made more good buddies with my fellow lawyers and agents making the *Newsies* deals than for any other show. And the same held true for my "clients"—the incredible team of my Disney colleagues, whom I did my best to support in the trenches those months. It was that kind of show and that sort of journey.

Cut to June 2012. It's Tony night. The Disney crew is all at a big viewing party at the Hard Rock Café, shell-shocked that we were there, optimistic that we'd take home a few of those critters. Best Score comes up. We win. My amazing colleague Jane Abramson, with whom I worked on all sorts of *Newsies* stuff, including all manner of music team negotiations, comes running up to me, jumps into my arms, and screams, "We won!" We all felt that sort of spirit—even the lawyers got a hug! Later that night a whole bunch of us went out to a bar in the Theater District to celebrate a bit more, to let the night go on for just a little bit longer. I'm chatting with my new buddy, Bob Duva, agent to the now Tony-winning genius of choreography, Chris Gattelli, one of the many with whom I made a deal "we can all live with," and Chris comes by. I give him a congratulatory hug, and Bob sneaks away his Tony. The camera snaps, and I have my favorite photo of the world, holding Chris's Tony on that amazing night.

Cut to the next day. All sorts of nice e-mails from friends. Best of all was a note from one of my younger friends, the first one to pester me when I joined Disney ("*Newsies* . . . when is it coming to Broadway?!?"). This time: "I waited 20 years to see *Newsies* on Broadway and was crying watching the Tony performance last night. Woo-hoo! Dreams come true." Being a little cog in the success of *Newsies* was amazing, watching all of us work at the top of our game was thrilling, and making lots of new friends—and holding one's Tony Award!—along the way was a lot of fun. But it was that note that meant the most to me. I think for all of us here, whether production assistant or president or just a lawyer like me, it's the love that people feel for this show that has made all the spitting and all the handshakes worth it.

Jeremy Jordan, John Dossett

Katie Carbone, Howell, NJ

Mackenzie Aladjem, Los Angeles, CA

Kym Buchly, Dallas, TX

"I've been a fan of *Newsies* since 1992. I remember the promotion for it was a newspaper with the cast pictures and bios. I kept that for YEARS afterwards. I loved the cast, the dancing, the music, everything. I nearly fell off my chair when I heard it was coming to Broadway. It still hasn't lost any of its magic."

— Jenn Ryan, Lancaster, PA

Samantha Shoop, Camp H

"Growing up, I knew I wanted to be a performer, but as I got older, I started to question it. I ended up at the Nederlander Theatre and my breath was taken away. I am now auditioning for everything I can and I hope to attend a performing arts college. Thank you for giving me the inspiration!"

— Darian Doom-DeVoto, Louisville, KY

"This past March, my husband and I took his students to see *Newsies*. I was so thrilled to be able to share this musical with a new generation and hoped they would fall in love with it as I did when I was their age. Seeing their faces light up with so much joy was priceless."

— Elyse Stevenson, Charlotte, NC

"Growing up, my twin sister and I watched *Newsies* all the time. We would sing and dance along with the movie. For Christmas, my sister surprised me with two tickets to New York City for our 26th birthday. I was so excited, I cried. And then the whole family cried. It was the best trip I have ever taken."

— Morgan Pratt, Richmond, VT

Rosanna Pagtakhan, Edison, NJ

Dana Sevean, Wayne, NJ

Amanda Croke, Stafford, VA

Melissa Rhees, Heber City, UT

Carolyn Tomlinson, Derry, PA

"In high school, my friends and I would blast the soundtrack from the original *Newsies* movie while we drove around town or got ready for a musical of our own. Of course, we sang along with fierce excitement! When we found out *Newsies* was going to be on Broadway, we were over the moon with ecstasy! From the beginning, we followed all the news articles and YouTube updates about the progress of the show and with each new development, we rejoiced."

— Sonnet Stockmar, Portland, OR

Alex Bishop, High Springs, FL

"*Newsies* really came full circle for me when in celebration of my mom's recent clean bill of health after facing breast cancer, our family took a trip to NYC to see the show. Little did I know that we were also going to be celebrating my engagement! My amazing fiancé and sister, with the help of the fabulous cast and crew, arranged a "tour" of backstage. Then to my surprise, on stage, I was handed a special signed Playbill as Jason dropped to one knee. We were cheered on by the cast in the audience and it will forever be one of the most memorable nights."

— Amanda McKenzie, Winston-Salem, NC

Amanda McKenzie, Winston-Salem, NC

The Sun.
NEWSIES STOP THE WORLD.
NIGHT EDITION
NIGHT EDITION

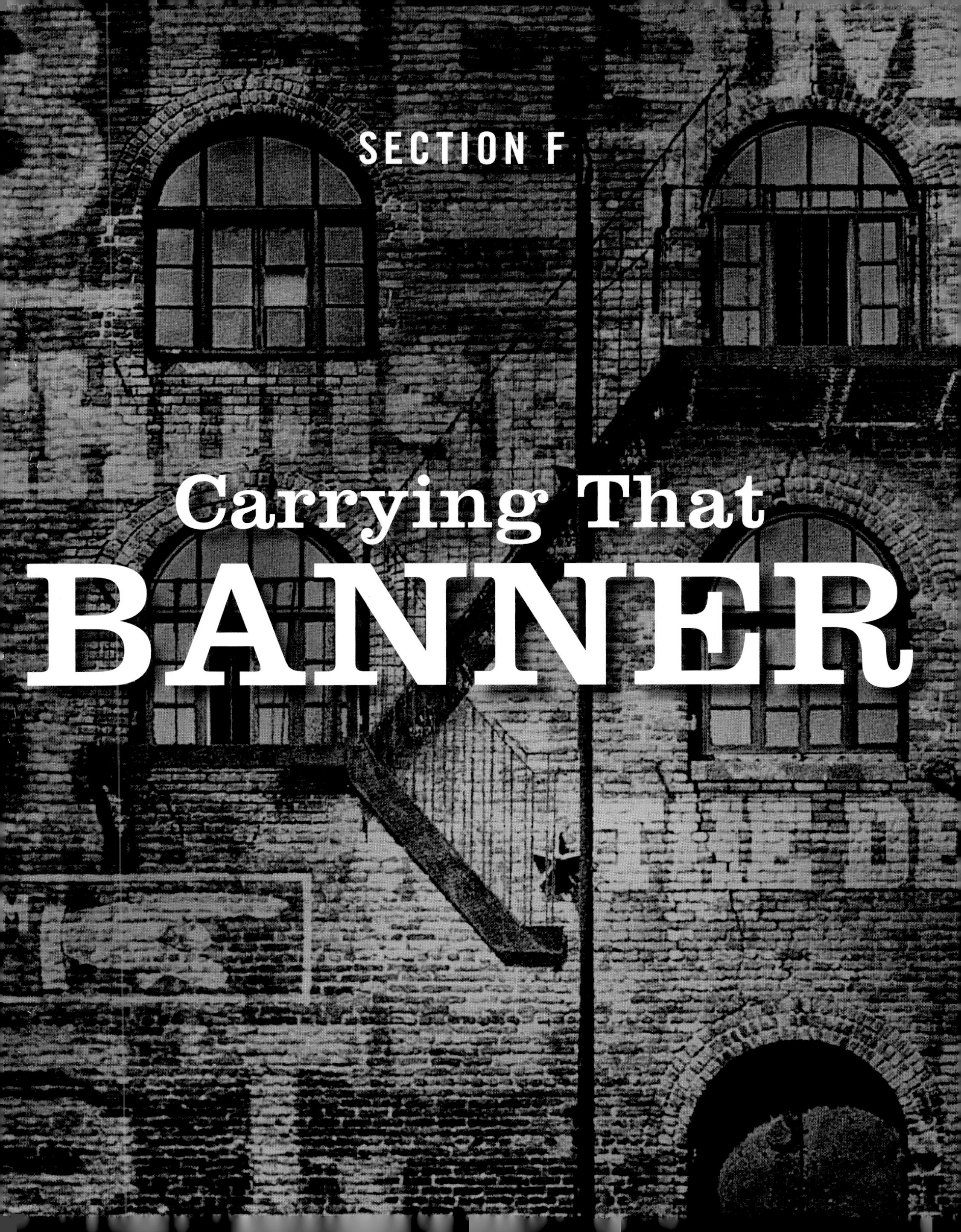

SECTION F

Carrying That BANNER

Following the Fansies

David Schrader
executive vice president
and managing director, DTG

Andrew Flatt
senior vice president of marketing, DTG

Bryan Dockett
vice president of sales, DTG

DAVID: Way back 10 or 15 years ago, I remember going to our old office in California and having conversations about what should we be developing. People in business affairs pulled out stacks of letters and said, "Can we look at *Newsies*?" For years, performers and people running amateur and professional theaters sent us letters asking about licensing *Newsies*. How often do people actually sit down and write a letter? But there wasn't a vetted stage musical form of *Newsies*, or any Disney musical for that matter, that we could license to anybody. Once we started licensing *Beauty and the Beast* through Music Theatre International in 2004, that put the idea back in people's heads. It took several more years before we had a show to put onstage, but even then nobody knew for sure how much energy to put into it. What did it want to be?

BRYAN: The first time I ever heard the title was in a meeting with Tom Schumacher. He said, "We're going to go experiment with *Newsies* out at Paper Mill Playhouse." I wrote down on my notepad, "What is *Newsies*?" I did not grow up with the movie and knew absolutely not a thing about it. But I looked it up and thought, "Hmm, that is an interesting storyline. Okay, let's see what happens!"

DAVID: We got to Paper Mill with the expectation of testing a licensable musical. Nobody was talking about Broadway. In the meantime, fans of the movie were chatting online: "Oh, I can't believe this is actually happening!"

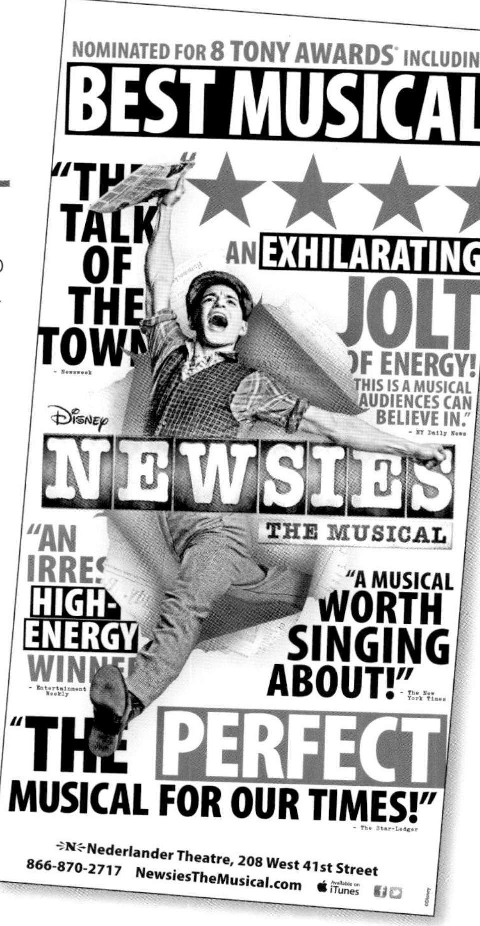

ANDREW: From the moment *Newsies* was first announced for Paper Mill Playhouse, there was a movement by the fans to bring it to Broadway. Soon this collective group became known as "Fansies." It is rare to have such a passionate following behind a show before it even hits the boards, but the voice of these spirited and loyal *Newsies* ambassadors on social media became a key factor in raising awareness around the production and establishing its credibility.

BRYAN: We reached out to five or six of our top Broadway sales partners and said, "Hey, we are testing this show in New Jersey. We are not bringing it to Broadway, but we'll take you to dinner and it will be a nice night out!" At intermission, they said, "Wow, this is actually pretty interesting. You guys should bring this to Broadway. We can sell this!" And I said, "Who can you sell it to?" "Oh, we can sell it to student groups." "That's great—one performance out of eight for the week. So thanks for helping me with that one!" But they were intrigued, as many of them actually knew about the movie and its following.

DAVID: The movie fans who made their way to Paper Mill seemed to like it even more than they thought they would and supported the stage musical, changes and all. Then we had a Broadway theater owner going out to Paper Mill to see it just because he thought it was a cool idea. During the show, he looked back at us saying, "Why aren't you transferring this? Look around. It is a real musical. People actually really like it." Now there was a different business decision in front of us. *Newsies* was doing well at Paper Mill, although it didn't really have time in three or four weeks to catch fire in terms of sales. But you could feel its potential in the theater. So we started looking to see what it would cost with the modest scale of the physical production, an available theater, and a limited run. This process was unusual for us, because we think we can plan every detail of everything five years ahead and we are never going to change our minds. But we did! The economics of it were pretty reasonable at first, because we felt that taking *Newsies* to Broadway would help license the show, legitimize it in a way that nobody expected. We said, "Let's just put it on sale for 12 weeks and see what happens."

BRYAN: When we first dug into sales, it was just going to be a limited run to support licensing. But we had never worked on a limited-run Disney production. So we said, "Let's line up as many ducks as we can and hit the 12 weeks, then it will close and we will go right back to *The Lion King* and *Mary Poppins*." We didn't get into extensive group buildup or embrace any international sales objectives that we would for any other production. We were just putting it out there. But the interesting thing was all the die-hard fans who came out of the woodwork and were the ones who told us that there was more to *Newsies* than just us. They helped build that whole base of folks who now enjoy the show every day.

DAVID: The Fansies were not the typical Broadway audience. They lived in 50 states, not within 50 miles, so I didn't know what was going to happen. We put the 12 weeks on sale, and I was shocked at the initial response. That was real. You could see the transactions and the chatter going at the same time. We could see them interacting on Facebook and Twitter—and they actually bought tickets. Think about what that means! I live in Nevada and I'm going to make plans to get to New York just to see this new show. That might happen for a famous title that hadn't been revived in 30 years. But no one had ever seen *Newsies* as a legitimate stage show before. To them it was just an idea. Before long, fans from all 50 states were flocking here—like Woodstock! You could totally feel in the theater that they were waiting for *Newsies* this whole time. They knew all the songs. And they were not necessarily the kids we thought they were going to be. If you knew the film from the theaters in 1992 or home video, you're now in your mid- to late 20s, your early 30s, or you're somebody in her 50s whose kid was obsessed. That was the mix we started seeing in the house.

BRYAN: When we put *Newsies* out there for the first 12 weeks, it sold really quickly. The Nederlander is a small house, which doesn't have a lot of upside with only 1,200 seats, and the location tucked out of the way on 41st Street doesn't get much walk-up traffic, but the grosses were impressive. We had no discounts in the marketplace, and people were even buying premium tickets! So we started looking at the next 10 weeks, which would put us into the summer, when the tourism flourishes and nearly every show on Broadway does really well. We figured there were more Fansies out there as well as regular theatergoers who were into great dancing. And at that time we were preparing for the Tonys—with eight nominations, we could win a couple of things, if not Best Musical. We were confident we could run *Newsies* until the end of the summer, so we put those additional 10 weeks on sale, and those flew out the door really quickly!

DAVID: After the 10-week extension sold, everyone was staring again, like, "Now what do we do? Do we put this in an open-ended run? Will it pivot from being largely fueled by Fansies to the broader population?"

BRYAN: Then we took the big leap. David's philosophy was the best: "Let's let it run and the fans will tell us when they've had enough." Still, it was a huge risk to open up the run, because we had no idea what was going to happen. We didn't do the normal buildup and had no

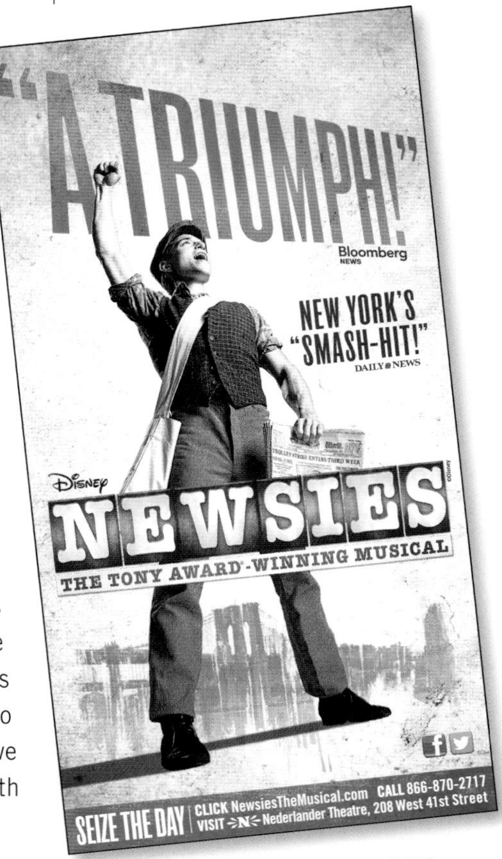

groups booked for the fall. Luckily, we had some groups who had raised their hand and said, "Hey, if you extend again—because we don't believe you it's limited—put us in."

ANDREW: With an open run to support, we had a big challenge: how to educate the "non-Fansie" public about what *Newsies* was and why they should go see it. For the uninitiated, the story of New York newsboys banding together to take down a publishing giant at the turn of the 20th century doesn't exactly sound like a typical night on Broadway. However, just as the newsies faced their challenge, so did our marketing team. To overcome this hurdle, the team continues to build campaigns around key moments in time to communicate the contemporary relevancy of the show with a goal of creating a larger impact on the soon-to-be ticket buyers.

The creative team and company celebrating one year on Broadway

DAVID: At one point, "*Newsies* Broadway" was trending on Yahoo. To be relevant at that level means that many people are suddenly talking about a stage show—a lot! It was like a news event, which made the media here pay attention to it. And I think media people are generally favorable to this show because it is about them—about the newspaper business and how it prevailed through this particular period in time and went on for a hundred years to be the source for news. So it wasn't us saying, "Hey, come pay attention to our great show," it was the Fansies and the audience saying, "Pay attention to this." At some point, the media had to at least write about the phenomenon that it was, which helped it cross over to a regular Broadway audience, and that is consistently what we have seen for a year.

ANDREW: In the first year, several campaigns were developed to speak directly to *Newsies* and its life on Broadway in a given moment in time. The "Catch NEWSIES Fever" campaign used a quote from *Entertainment Weekly* to express the excitement of fans in the show's first few months onstage. As the fan base grew, the message evolved to deliver a fresh yet consistent message. At the one-year anniversary, a celebratory campaign featuring a snippet from a review in Bloomberg News perfectly underscored the show's success on Broadway as well as the success of the strike of the newsies themselves: "A triumph!" was painted on everything from buses to billboards across New York City. Strong and defiant newsies splashed across the city and brought the energy of the production off the stage and into the streets.

BRYAN: Like any show, we had a couple of periods in the fall and the winter that were a little tough. But we made it through. We have made money every single week and recouped the Broadway transfer in only forty weeks—the fastest for any Disney show. And we've been fortunate to have attracted specialty groups that are not typical for our other shows. For example, we have a lot of dance groups. When both young and older dancers see Christopher Gattelli's choreography and the high energy of our cast, they go crazy. And then there's the Fansies. I never could have imagined the depth of their passion for *Newsies*, even to this day. When they still come, they let you know they are having a great time. The energy in that theater every single day is fascinating. There is not a person who leaves the show without a smile on their face.

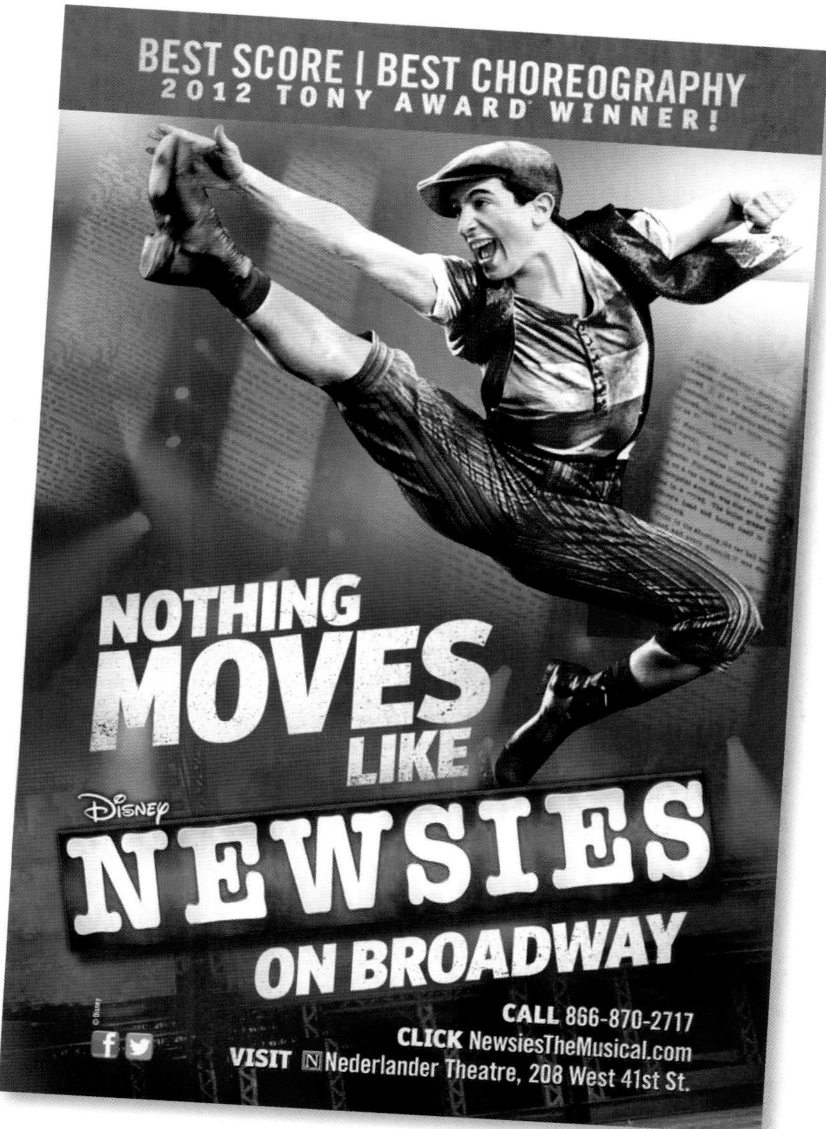

ANDREW: As we have settled into the Nederlander Theatre, the Fansies have continued to surprise with their love and support for the show and its powerful message. Developing compelling content that would take them (and subsequently, their networks) behind the curtain became a key focus in the marketing strategy for *Newsies*. A series of backstage videos started to feed into YouTube with the help of cast member Andrew Keenan-Bolger. His unique take gave an honest and genuine look behind the scenes in a way no other Broadway production had before. Memes, GIFs, and tweets began to make the rounds online, growing the Fansies to hundreds of thousands. Together, these tools allowed *Newsies* to become more than a musical, but a living, breathing community that developed its own place in today's culture.

DAVID: Here we are, sitting at the Tony Awards a year after the show opened, and there are only two musicals from last season—*Once* and *Newsies*—that somehow found an audience and got through. And when you see *Newsies* on the Tony Awards, it seems perfectly natural at this point that they are a part of the fabric of Broadway as much as anybody else is. Half a million people have now seen the show on Broadway. It totally is "The Little Engine That Could"—one of those things that nobody can reverse engineer what would make that work. Step-by-step, *Newsies* just sort of confounded and surprised us. You can't plan for that to happen. And it echoes what happens in the musical. A group of people got together and spread the word—now in a 21st-century way—and got people excited about something. Nobody told them they had to do it. It was just crowd sourcing, "What would I like to see on Broadway?" And suddenly there it is!

ON FACEBOOK! MORE THAN 5.8 MILLION PEOPLE ARE REACHED BY 5,500 PEOPLE POSTING ON *NEWSIES*' FIRST ANNIVERSARY

▼ Broadway Cares Easter Bonnet, 2013 ▲ Signing souvenir posters

▲ Real newsie Robert Spellman (middle)

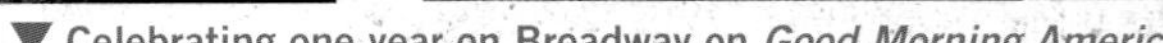

▲ Kara Lindsay, Jeremy Jordan ▼ Celebrating one year on Broadway on *Good Morning America*

▼ Sherri Shepherd, Tom Schumacher

▲ Paper Mill cast, November 24, 2011

▲ Macy's Thanksgiving Day Parade

▼ John Dossett, Bernadette Peters

▲ Lou Castro

▲ *OK*! magazine, October 8, 2012

▼ Celebrating high school graduation on the stage of the Nederlander Theatre

Disney
NEWSIES
THE MUSICAL
KATHERINE

Disney
NEWSIES
THE MUSICAL
ALBERT

Disney
NEWSIES
THE MUSICAL
OSCAR DELANCEY

Disney
NEWSIES
THE MUSICAL
ROMEO

Disney
NEWSIES
THE MUSICAL
SPECS

Disney
NEWSIES
THE MUSICAL
ELMER

Disney
NEWSIES
THE MUSICAL
SNIPER

Disney
NEWSIES
THE MUSICAL
SPOT CONLON

Disney
NEWSIES
THE MUSICAL
KNOBS

Disney
NEWSIES
THE MUSICAL
BUTTONS

Disney
NEWSIES
THE MUSICAL
MUSH

Disney
NEWSIES
THE MUSICAL
BARNEY PEANUTS

Disney
NEWSIES
THE MUSICAL
HENRY

Disney
NEWSIES
THE MUSICAL
RACE

Disney
NEWSIES
THE MUSICAL
FINCH

Disney
NEWSIES
THE MUSICAL
JO JO

The Art of the Souvenir

Steve Downing
vice president of merchandise, DTG

We don't know what we don't know until we don't do what we normally do. From the very beginning, this mantra inspired our work with *Newsies* and challenged us to be creative in a nontraditional way. We couldn't get away with playing it safe or following in others' footsteps—not even our own. Because of the unique enthusiasm surrounding *Newsies*' transfer to Broadway, audiences needed to be wowed from the second they walked up to the Nederlander Theatre until they made their way out of the show with newly purchased souvenirs. We spent countless hours imagining, creating, and refining the merchandise, because at the end of the day, the items that went home with guests would embody their theatergoing memories forever.

For every Disney Theatrical show, we had created a glossy souvenir brochure that attempted to capture the essence of the stage experience in photos and text. But for *Newsies*, we stepped outside our conventional mold and instead created a souvenir newspaper, which allowed us to offer the best production shots and the most comprehensive information on the show in a cost-effective and *Newsies* kind of way. This innovation extended to the merchandise kiosk, where one creative spark ignited the next. Why not sell newspapers and merchandise from a newspaper stand? And why couldn't our merchandise team become newsies themselves? And if our staff could become newsies, why not also our audience members, who loved the show just as much as we did? We wanted to make sure that every person who came to *Newsies* could take a piece of it home and become part of the team. A newsie cap, tote bag, or T-shirt isn't just a piece of merchandise—it's a chance for theatergoers to become a part of the show and to show the world they saw *Newsies*. We were thrilled to see that sales for *Newsies* souvenirs came fast and furious, exceeding all expectations!

Since the Fansies are such an integral part of the show's success, we wanted to create something special that could engage their enthusiasm and help launch the show (and our young cast) on Broadway. Limited-edition, collectible *Newsies* trading cards that comprised every newsboy in the original cast and their young advocate, Katherine, opened the doors for actors and audiences to connect outside the performance. The cast was ecstatic to get individual stacks of custom cards to sign and distribute at the stage door. Fans quickly took to social media to get "code words" from actors and connect with each other about their cards and when they were going back to the show for more! This dialogue among cast and fans is what *Newsies* is all about: inclusion, creativity, shattering the norms, and becoming a community. The fact that our innovations with merchandise have played a key role in helping *Newsies* connect with audiences makes me think that perhaps we shouldn't ever do what we normally do.

COVERING NEW YORK DAILY
MORNING EDITION

The New York Sun

ONE CENT

NEWSIES STOP THE WORLD

A MODERN DAY DAVID IS POISED TO TAKE ON THE RICH AND POWERFUL GOLIATH
With the swagger of one twice his age, armed with nothing more than a few nuggets of truth, Jack Kelly stands ready to face the behemoth Pulitzer.

DAVID VS. GOLIATH AT THE BRINK OF A NEW CENTURY

By K. Plumber

With all eyes fixed on the trolley strike, there's another battle brewing in the city. A modern-day David is poised to take on the rich and powerful Goliath. With the swagger of one twice his age, armed with nothing more than a few nuggets of truth, Jack Kelly stands ready to face the behemoth Pulitzer. In the words of union leader Kelly, "We will work with you. We will even work for you. But we will be paid and treated as valuable members of your organizations." Then he addressed the boys whom Pulitzer recruited as scabs: "For the sake of all the kids in every sweatshop, factory, and slaughter house in New York, I beg you... join us."

NEDERLANDER THEATER

Opened on September 1, 1921, and originally named The National Theatre, The Nederlander Theatre has been home to some of the greatest plays and musicals in Broadway history. Lillian Hellman's "The Little Foxes" made Tallulah Bankhead a star in 1939. "Inherit the Wind" headlined Paul Muni and Ed Begley in 1955 and Edward Albee's "Who's Afraid of Virginia Woolf?" premiered 1962. The theatre was renamed for David M. Nederlander in 1980.

The New Musical 'Newsies' Features Music by Alan Menken, Lyrics by Jack Feldman, and Book by Harvey Fierstein

JACK KELLY

An Unlikely Star Is Born
By K. Plumber

Picture a handsome, heroically charismatic, plain spoken, know-nothing, skirt-chasing, cocky little flirt – a complete egomaniac. The fact is he's also the face of the strike. What a face! Face the fact: that's a face that could save us all from sinking in the ocean. Give those kids and me the brand new century and watch what happens! It's David and Goliath, do or die, the fight is on and I can't watch what happens. But all I know is nothing happens if you just give in. It can't be any worse than how it's been. And it just so happens that we just might win. So whatever happens, let's begin!

OFFICAL NEWSIES CAP

Creating a Record for Posterity

LEFT: Alan Menken, Frank Filipetti
OPPOSITE (CLOCKWISE FROM TOP LEFT): Garett Hawe, Thayne Jasperson, Andy Richardson; Matthew Schechter, Lewis Grosso; Capathia Jenkins; Kara Lindsay; John Dossett; Andrew Keenan-Bolger; Jeremy Jordan

Kurt Deutsch
cast recording producer

I have a long relationship with Tom Schumacher, going back to when my wife, Sherie, was in *Aida*, which Disney produced right around that time we started our record label, Ghostlight/Sh-K-Boom. Tom and Disney Theatrical were very supportive of us from the very beginning—I think we were the first label that Disney allowed to sell solo records in the lobby. Throughout the years, as I've gone from solo records to cast albums, I've been keeping Tom apprised of my unique business model, and I kept hoping that one day we could do this together. When *Newsies* came around, Tom said, "Maybe this is the time."

When I first saw the show at Paper Mill, I honestly didn't know what to expect, but the energy, choreography, song arrangements, and Jeremy's performance . . . they were very exciting! *Newsies* has these anthems for boys that, if I were to have heard as a kid growing up in St. Louis, would have inspired me to dream about singing these songs on Broadway, performing them in high school, or just being part of the theater. There are not a lot of shows geared toward young boys. *Pippin* was the one for me. *Newsies* is different from *Pippin*, but it has that feeling. This is the music that I would listen to.

Our independent label focuses on the niche of Broadway cast albums. We've now been doing it for 10 years and have about 150 albums. We are part of the theater community, which we care about deeply, and are all here wanting to make Broadway as good as it can be. From the beginning, I've tried to represent new musicals and the new generation of Broadway. To me, *Newsies* really fit in with shows like *Spelling Bee* and *Legally Blonde* and *Next to Normal* and *The Drowsy Chaperone* and *In the Heights*. It feels new and exciting and not your grandma's Broadway. *Newsies* is in many ways an old-fashioned musical, but it is young. It's the kids who want to sing it. I was picking my son up from summer camp, and the camp chorus was singing songs from *Newsies*—all these boys singing "Seize the Day." Even though *Newsies* has a traditional Broadway feel, it still resonates with youth.

The album is doing very well—in context, of course. We are in a microscopic business with only about 8,000 people seeing the show each week. It's not like a big TV show or film with millions of viewers. Cast recordings are long-tail investments, because, unlike the original production, the recording lasts forever. Without a cast recording, it is as if the musical never existed.

For me, it is about preservation. Listening to the album is like reading a book, because if you haven't seen the production, you can at least imagine what those performances were like onstage. It's a big responsibility that I don't take lightly.

Seizing the Learning Opportunity

Lisa Mitchell
education & outreach manager, DTG

When *Newsies* was gearing up for its limited Broadway engagement, it didn't make much sense to put the time, money, or effort into creating our usual array of educational programs or materials. Sure, the show was a rich springboard for learning across content areas, and, yes, the dramatized local history was built into area curriculum, making the show an educational gold mine for teachers. But there was one teeny-tiny problem: the limited engagement was scheduled to begin on March 15 and conclude on June 10. While a few schools were bound to come in the late spring before school let out, for the most part budgets were spent up, school calendars were locked, and few new field trips were likely to be added to the books. Even if the show extended its run, it would certainly conclude in the summer, before school was back in session. In other words, the educational materials and experiences would be built for naught.

So putting the time, research, money, and effort into building out learning opportunities despite the logical conclusion not to was either profoundly stupid or a leap of faith. Regardless, it took some crafty maneuvering to make it happen. But happen it did, and when an open-ended run was announced, the DTG education team was at the ready with a fully realized curriculum and engaging group-workshop content. Here's a little story about how we did it, why we did it, and what makes learning through *Newsies* engaging, enriching, and unlike anything else we've done.

Sell the Headline. Sometimes you have to spin the story to sell it to the right people. Though we were crossing fingers, toes, and eyes that *Newsies* would become an open-ended run, the powers that be were keeping mum and it seemed that even an extension was unlikely. But if there was even an inkling of a chance of the show continuing in the fall, there just had to be an amazing study guide and workshop. So here in the education department we told our colleagues that we'd have to build these things anyway to accompany our ultimate licensing materials. Might as well get a head start on it. Yeah, that's it.

Seize the Staff. Given the show's unlikely future, educational content had to be created efficiently. There is a wealth of history buffs in our office, and our ace creative services team was willing to handle study guide design in-house. The creation of the guide did take up a chunk of overhead time, but it saved a bundle in outsourcing expenses, too. So we divided and conquered. Brendan Padgett in our publicity department had done exhaustive research several years ago as our literary intern, and his MFA in dramaturgy was also a huge help, so he dug into child labor and reform. Colleen McCormack, our creative development coordinator, headed up New York and world history at the turn of the 20th century. Elizabeth Boulger, creative development assistant, took point on everything about the show itself: a synopsis, character descriptions, and background on the creative team. Everyone researched and wrote illuminating articles on their areas. My job was to fold their work into an experiential curriculum, tie it to the show, and align everything with educational standards. We dove into the Library of Congress and found some fascinating historical photos and newspaper articles. My favorite discovery was a reporter's account of the newsboys' rally . . . the journalist singles out two women in the room as reporters from *The Sun*. Wow. Katherine was real! Tom Schumacher saw that Kara Lindsay had a copy of the article in her dressing room that night.

Make Changes, Once and For All. Newsies dramatizes serious and politically charged issues: child labor, unions, class, power, and reform. The content of the show gave us an opportunity to meet these issues head-on in a way that we hadn't before—our previous shows hadn't examined such polarizing content. We decided to embrace this challenge and wrote the curriculum so that the learner could draw her own conclusions on subjects like bias, organized labor, and class. Kids respond to *Newsies* because it is a story about them. While the fictional newsboys in our musical are teenagers, the historical newsies were often much younger. Oppressed kids ages seven to 17 really suffered, really fought, and really earned a fair compromise. Our curricu-

Christopher Gattelli instructing teaching artists

"Seize the Day" workshop

lum had to honor that struggle. But treading closely to heated issues meant we had to set up the educator for success. We overhauled our study guide format to provide the teacher with fully realized, step-by-step lesson plans to guide her through this difficult subject matter and ensured that healthy reflection time was built into the process.

Hold a Rally. With the study guide taking shape, it was time to call in the troops. Our Broadway workshops are available to groups from around the world who book tickets through our in-house ticketing team. For *Mary Poppins*, kids learned the music and movement to "Supercalifragilisticexpialidocious"; for *The Lion King*, they explore the African chants and rhythms of the Pridelands. With a limited engagement for *Newsies*, there was no compelling business reason to build a group workshop. But we had one interested group, and an opportunity to participate in an education event with the New-York Historical Society. The one interested group was booked for a workshop on March 18. *Newsies* began previews on March 15. On March 16, first thing in the morning, the morning after the first preview, choreographer Christopher Gattelli got up early and made the time to teach the Disney teaching artists the choreography from "Seize the Day." They'd have one day to learn it well enough to re-teach it to our first group of kids. Chris could have taken one look at the room of arts educators and opted to teach them an easier number from the show. Or he could have modified the "Seize the Day" dance to be more accessible to the nondancers in the room. Both would have been reasonable concessions. Instead, he addressed the teaching artists as peers and shared his vision of the building of "Jack's army." He taught them the full choreography, just as it is performed eight times a week by the most skilled and disciplined dancers on Broadway. He was kind and gentle and believed they could do it. And they did it.

Watch What Happens. On March 18, our teaching artists taught their very first *Newsies* workshop to a group of adolescent dancers from Pennsylvania. Just as Chris did for them, the teaching artists took the kids through the unmodified choreography from "Seize the Day." And just as the teaching artists did with Chris, the kids rose to the occasion and learned the dance. Imagine their faces as they got to the matinee and realized, "We just did that!" That is what is different about teaching and learning through *Newsies*. Every step of the way the bar has been held high, and students have exceeded expectations.

On May 19, 2012, an open-ended run was finally announced. With workshops and curriculum at the ready, kids have been learning through the show ever since. For *Newsies* alone, we doubled our number of workshop participants by the show's first anniversary in 2013—we taught twice as many kids *Newsies* in half a year as we did for *Mary Poppins* and *The Lion King* combined for all of 2012. In her act-one solo, Katherine sings, "Give those kids and me the brand new century and watch what happens." The content of *Newsies* and the heart of the people who created it have shown us what can happen. Kids can form considered opinions and conquer challenging material when given the chance, and an unlikely musical about unlikely heroes can inspire a generation.

What It Takes to Do *Newsies* Eight Shows a Week

Justin Huff

As I worked to cast both developmental readings, the Paper Mill production, the original Broadway company, and subsequent replacements, I have often been asked what it takes to be a newsie. Of course, it takes the raw talent and skill to perform this high-octane show eight times a week. However, I believe that the most important answer is the desire to be part of something bigger than yourself. During our auditions for Paper Mill, I remember Ryan Steele, Thayne Jasperson, Jess LeProtto, and so many more who embodied the raw strength and passion that the boys must possess. So much of who our newsies are onstage is a direct reflection of who the actors are offstage. It's that mentality of teamwork that makes the collaboration they share onstage every night so inspiring.

The *Newsies* ensemble accepting the Actors' Equity Award for Outstanding Broadway Chorus

Michael Fatica

Being a newsie really is all it's cracked up to be. Every night onstage, we are instantly thrust into a fraternity of the most amazing 17 brothers a boy could ask for. The camaraderie this show allows is something I have never experienced before and don't know if I ever will again. These characters are fighting for their livelihood and the right to have a voice, something not any one boy could do on his own at the turn of the 20th century. As swings for this show, we get to experience this fight from 14 different sets of eyes, which has only made this experience richer. Each character has such amazing personal relationships, and we are encouraged to create our own. For example, as Tommy Boy, I get picked on relentlessly (that means you, Jack Kelly) but have been granted the nickname Scrappy-Doo as a Delancey. Every newsie has his own distinct view of the strike and why he is agreeing to risk his life for it. Chris gave us the imagery of carrying a sword to charge into battle. His choreography is inspiring on so many levels and helps us tell the story by literally leaping through the streets for our rights. With every performance, we have the opportunity to find a new part of ourselves that needs to fight for freedom and in turn learn something new about ourselves.

Aaron Albano

It's so easy in *Newsies* to do flashy choreography, a million turns, and kick your face. Chris is brilliant because he allows us to do that but focuses us in the right way to tell the story. Every time we have a brush-up rehearsal, he always says, "I love that you guys can do these amazing things, but that's not what it's about."

Mark Hummel

Eight shows a week, week after week, is fun, but it's also work. Occasionally, I do have to encourage the 12 members of our ace orchestra, who for a particular performance might "just play" in the pit. I say, "Oh-no. That's not what the cast is doing up onstage. They're dancing for their lives in this musical. The orphans sing and dance their thoughts and emotions or they'll die. We've got to play like that because it has to match." I remind them that every night is opening night: people are paying big bucks and they may only be coming once. We've got to

What Makes a "Good Scene"?

LaVon Fisher-Wilson, Ben Fankhauser, Matthew Schechter

Tom Murray
musician

The most common question one Broadway pit musician asks another Broadway pit musician about a particular show is, "How's the scene over there?" or "Is it a good scene?" What constitutes a "good scene" is a combination of elements, all of which are found in *Newsies*.

First, there's the music: the compositions themselves. There's no better Broadway composer today than Alan Menken. In recent history, his only equals are Stephen Sondheim and Andrew Lloyd Webber. We're talking about a Gershwin, Hammerstein, Porter, Arlen, or Berlin of our time! Alan's melodies, harmonies, counterlines, and use of themes (modulated through different keys and tempos) are so well crafted, the result is emotionally moving music that has a purity and simplicity to it. For example, "Something to Believe In," "Seize the Day," and "Santa Fe" all seem so natural and flow so gracefully it's as though they have always existed. This is the genius of Alan Menken.

Another element of a "good scene" is excellent in *Newsies*: orchestrations and music supervision. Danny Troob and Michael Kosarin have worked with Alan on many hit shows and they work seamlessly together. These guys decide who plays what instrument when; what instrument has the melody, countermelody, or background; in what range it should be played; and at what dynamic level to best enhance the scene and lyric happening onstage. Whether it's solo trumpet at the opening of the show, old-style jazzy violin, screaming rock guitar, or the intimate sound of solo clarinet or cello, the right choices in orchestration give texture and depth to the entire production. They also make us musicians feel good, because we know we're contributing to the show in a meaningful way.

What's a "scene" without the cats in the band? John Miller put the *Newsies* orchestra together. He is the guru of musical contractors because he is so sensitive not only to the abilities of musicians but also to our personalities. How will these musicians get along eight times a week in close quarters? The result is the *Newsies* orchestra. Great playing! Great hang! Lots of love in this pit. We have one member so devoted to the group that she brought her own mop in from home to wipe up spills at the water cooler!

Finally, you have the conductor. He sets the tenor, or vibe, for the whole experience and inspires us to play with gusto show after show. He is our moral compass, a beacon who guides us on many a stormy night safely to the exit music. Mark Hummel shines! Always smiling. Always grooving. Always enthusiastic. (He's also a very snappy dresser and regularly brings us candy and flowers!)

Add great stage and company management, theater staff, crew, supportive producers, well-executed marketing, and twin newsies from my hometown (David and Jacob Guzman), and you've got a "great scene" and a fine life!

The Rise – and Fall – of a Prop

Brendon Stimson
Oscar Delancey

Many actors in *Newsies* use a myriad of props during the show. In my own track, for example, I use a rag, dice, a rope, the "Flushing" sign, my favorite brass knuckles, and, of course, Ike's broom. (Ike is the newsie I play when I'm not Oscar.) Now, most of these props won't ever need a replacement (unless I roll the dice down the manhole again . . .). But, as we found out over 50 performances into the run, brooms are breakable. Once that first broom broke, I took myself down memory lane to trace back when I first met and used it.

It all stems back to a small presentation of "King of New York" that a few of us newsies did in between the Paper Mill production and Broadway. We had made a condensed version and were prepped to perform it on the Nederlander stage (our first time ever being on the stage). Now, I had only used a big broom back at Paper Mill, and that prop belonged to the theater and did not transfer with us. We arrived to rehearse the number onstage and quickly realized we had no broom. No sweep-sweep! With not much time before our little performance, our fearless leader, Eduardo Castro, disappeared for about five minutes and searched every supply closet he could find for a suitable broom for this presentation. Victorious, he returned with broom in hand and saved the day. I practiced once with it, said "She'll do," and we were off. It was a slightly smaller broom than I was used to and had a bright yellow neck. It was perfect. The presentation went off without a hitch and everyone was pumped and buzzing about *Newsies*. I figured my experience with the small yellow broom was over.

Well, my friends, the broom got a nice paint job and had some more bristles attached. Not only did that broom last that one special performance, it lasted all of rehearsal, every preview, opening night, and just over 50 performances of *Newsies* on Broadway. One fateful performance, I was extra exuberant in the broom dance and busted the base area where the bristles met as well as snapped the top of the neck. It had been a good run, and the prototype for all brooms to come. To commemorate the first broom's memory and Ike, stage manager Tim Eaker and I did a photo shoot in the alley outside the theatrer. Hold your props close, people—you never know when they'll break.

Garett Hawe, Kara Lindsay, Brendon Stimson, Thayne Jasperson

The cast performing on *Dancing with the Stars*

deliver. That's our job. Any less is unacceptable in my book.

Alex Wong

When we moved into the Nederlander, I was seated beside Tommy Bracco in the dressing room. That was when I found my newsies twin. Tommy and I would always be laughing at something that none of the other guys were laughing at. Or talking about something ridiculous that only we thought was funny. *Newsies* became my home, and the offstage chemistry became onstage chemistry. We were newsboy friends onstage, having each other's back, and it honestly didn't feel any different offstage. I thought it was going to be difficult doing eight shows a week—and, yes, it was hard—but it's so enjoyable to sing and dance your heart out for an enthusiastic, sold-out crowd every night. Not only that, but I got to listen to Jeremy belt his face off, hear Ben's amazing riffs backstage, sit with Thayne in front of fans like puppies to dry off, roughhouse with Breslin, see Mike Faist step on a chair and have his leg go right through (and all the newsies frantically go to rescue him in the middle of "King of New York"), watch Kara launch a broomstick right into the orchestra pit, and then to top it all off, see Eduardo with a big supportive smile after the show as we went outside to sign Playbills for enthusiastic Fansies! Could it really get any better?

Ken Travis

You can't assume you are always going to get that amazing Fansie audience. The rule that we have is: don't mix the show that is not there. You can't force it. If the actors are tired, if it is the eighth show of the week, if we have a substitute musician, or anything that could make it odd—like a really quiet audience and the cast has to push hard to try to make it land or pull back because they are shocked by the silence—we can only mix the show we have. If you try to force it in the mix, the audience picks up on an energy difference. I'll get calls from Cassy or Gabe saying, "Hey, we had a couple of weird shows in a row. Come and take a listen. I need a fresh set of ears." Usually we can fix it in one sit-

Capathia Jenkins, Jeremy Jordan, and Kara Lindsay with Anika Noni Rose

through, because the team is so good. One funny thing that can happen is dialogue creeping up, usually because a joke won't have landed a couple of days in a row. Inevitably you feel like you made a mistake, so you will start mixing the scene hotter to make the laughs land. And sometimes it is just a couple of audiences in a row who don't think something's funny. Then I'll come watch and say, "Whoa, why is this scene so loud? There are only two people onstage!" And they're like, "Oh, right..." But these guys are so good—one of the best teams around. We laugh because the show reports always say, "The show sounds great out front."

Stuart Zagnit

None of the actors I covered missed shows early on in the run. So, as a swing covering the five adult male tracks, I was basically sitting by, waiting and watching. There were a lot of costume changes to learn, and also those set moves. You can take notes, but you only really learn by doing. Because of the tonnage onstage, you have to have a feel for how much pressure you need to apply to move that wagon across the stage. Early on, I'd get the momentum going and think, "Now I have to put the brakes on because I have to stop it!" That was challenging. So was the fight, because I am a lefty. When I'm doing Nick Sullivan's track, I have to remember to use the stick in the same hand as Nick (a righty), because it affects how he relates to the other characters. So I've had to become ambidextrous. As one of the newbies, certainly for the first couple of times I went on, I felt a lot of support. Everybody wanted me to succeed and that made that job a lot easier. This is truly an ensemble piece. We all work together as one unit, every night. And that makes a big difference. I give Jeff and Chris a lot of credit for setting the bar high.

Capathia Jenkins

Medda Larkin

My time at *Newsies* was joyous. I loved being with the young cast and a few of us "oldsies" thrown in for good measure. I laughed every day with the cast, crew, orchestra, management, and front-of-house staff. I wanted to be there no matter what—allergies, a headache, or just bone tired. I wanted to see those faces and laugh at those jokes and cry if I was so moved. I hadn't felt like this in a long time and for that I am so grateful. What an honor to have been in the original Broadway cast and all that comes with that. But what I hold most dear to my heart are the moments we all shared together as a company. Newsies forever!

LaVon Fisher-Wilson

Medda Larkin

I remember the day I was scheduled to audition for *Newsies*: I had just spent the weekend at a swimming party/sleepover with over 50 toddlers, so not only was my energy nonexistent, but also I had caught a cold from my youngest child, sending my voice into Barry White-land. I didn't feel well and was just about to skip the audition when my mom said, "Take some Mucinex, drink lots of water, and go and do your best." That was great advice, because what an adventure this has been! Never in my wildest dreams could I have imagined a role opening up a whole new level of performing for me and an amazing family to play with eight shows a week! But it was scary at first. I mean, here I am in a role that requires me to belt my face off and be consistent about it. I thought, "Could I do it?" I'd been on Broadway before as a swing, standby, and/or filled the role for three months, but this time, it would be all mine, all the time! So every day for the first few months, I was steaming my throat every chance I got, warming up and down, practicing not only my song in its original form but also a "B" version just in case my voice was weird. I didn't want to let the cast and those who hired me down! This role has taught me that nobody's voice is the same every day, but if I just go with the flow, stay confident, and do my best, I'll be successful.

Lou Castro

Now that we're open, we're a well-oiled machine. We go into work expecting to work hard, play hard, and sweat hard, because we truly love what we do. I've never had this much fun on one project. I feel somewhat spoiled. I am currently going around the country trying to hand-select dancers in auditions. When we say, "Welcome to the *Newsies* auditions," the roar that happens in the room tells me that the movie did one thing to inspire my generation, but the musical is now generating and inspiring a new breed of dancers. They are studying their craft just to be a part of this show and this industry. It's bigger than us. We're just a little side story. The auditions inspire them to take a tap class, to study singing, to go see theater, etc. I love that. In a way, I feel like we are doing what Bob and Noni did by sending their message out on the screen. People called the movie a failure, but I don't. It's not a failure because it changed my life. It changed so many people's lives.

Mark Hummel

Some of the show's energy no doubt comes from all the Broadway debuts. We've had 25 so far. My associate, Steven Malone, who's been with the show since Paper Mill, is a wonderful teacher, and I really appreciate his work and collaboration. He teaches the score and I do the final put-ins for the actors. I've noticed that there's a difference between those who are in high school and those who are in college. Those years are illuminating, with more life experience and training, clearly. We always encourage the younger ones to audition, but we have to pull stuff out of them a little more. When I see dead eyes, I know they don't really know what they're saying, so I'll take them aside and coach them about a lyric. It is a learning process and they learn from the audience, who need to care about them. And I've seen remarkable growth among those younger cast members. But there are so many talented actors up there. Ben Fankhauser is a really good actor and singer. And Davey is a tough role that he does so effortlessly. I watch it every single night, and both he and Corey as Jack Kelly try things and keep it ephemeral, live theater. It's happening right now, right in front of you, and it won't ever happen that way again. That's exciting.

Ben Fankhauser

A year into our Broadway run, I feel like I'm a completely different Davey now from when I started. We've hit 500 performances and you have no choice but to grow after doing the role eight times a week. When we first meet the new kid Davey, he's pretty timid. But after having done the show so much, it's sometimes a challenge for me to walk on that stage and see it like it's the first time. So if I'm having a difficult show, I can always grasp onto the fact that Davey needs to be there for his younger brother, Les. My experience with my brother helped me in this role—he is seven years older, which is also the age difference between Davey and Les. Not only is Davey helping to lead the strike and finding his own way,

Handstand competition with Olympic Gold Medalist Gabby Douglas (with red boots)

That Old Printing Press in the Cellar

Stuart Zagnit

When you are amusing yourself backstage, sometimes you come up with "songs that would have been cut from the show"—that is, fake cut songs. Near the end of the show, in Pulitzer's office, when they are trying to figure out who could have printed *The Newsies Banner*, Seitz says, "That old printing press in the cellar." So I wrote a song called "That Old Printing Press in the Cellar," which does nothing to move the show along. Everything would stop—because Mark Aldrich has a beautiful tenor voice—and in a "bad" version of *Newsies*, he would have had this little number about the old printing press, a metaphor for anyone who falls into the category of "oldsie":

Act Two, Scene Seven. Pulitzer's office.

PULITZER
I demand to know who defied my ban on printing strike material!

JACK
We're your loyal employees. We'd never take our business elsewhere.

SEITZ
That old printing press in the cellar . . .

Bell tone. Everyone freezes, except SEITZ, who sings:

THAT OLD PRINTING PRESS IN THE CELLAR,
THE ONE THAT THEY TOSSED LONG AGO,
TOO OLD AND OUTDATED TO SELL HER,
SO DOWN TO THE BASEMENT SHE'D GO.

Printing press at Woodside Press, Brooklyn, NY

BUT ONCE SHE WAS SHINY AND USEFUL,
SHE CRANKED OUT THE PAPES EV'RY DAY,
SOME INK AND SOME GREASE KEPT HER HUMMIN',
TILL ONE DAY THEY SENT HER AWAY.

THE YEARS THEY FLEW BY LIKE A WHIRLWIND,
AND PRESSES LIKE HER ARE PASSÉ,
TILL JACK AND HIS BOYS CAME A-CALLIN',
NOW SHE'S BACK AND SHE'S SEIZIN' THE DAY!

SO DON'T EVER COUNT OUT AN OLDSIE,
DON'T LAUGH 'CAUSE THEY'RE CREAKY AND GRAY,
YOU NEED NOT BE YOUNG TO HAVE VALUE,
DON'T LET THEM JUST TOSS YOU AWAY.

THAT OLD PRINTING PRESS IN THE CELLAR,
THE ONE THAT THEY TOSSED LONG AGO,
IT SWIRLED FOR THE WORLD LIKE A SOLDIER,
IT'S TIME THAT THE WORLD OUGHT TO KNOW!

but also he has to teach his brother how to be a respectable young man, which makes him very human. There's something very real about having a kid next to me who sometimes gets distracted. I have to watch out for him because that's what an older brother would do in any situation. But these kids are pros—some of them have done more Broadway shows than I have!

The other great thing that's happened recently is getting to do the show with Corey Cott, with whom I have been friends since very early in high school. (Jeremy and I have had a special bond over Ithaca College, but when he got *Smash* and it looked like things were really going to take off for him, Corey was cast to be his standby.) I thought it was unbelievable that we were going to even be in the same Broadway show. When Corey took over the role at the end of the summer, it was surreal. It is incredible to have known him for so long and then get to live out our childhood dreams together on Broadway. The last production we did together was *Rent*. I was Mark and he was Roger. Now, we're playing opposite each other once again—and in the Nederlander Theatre, where the original Broadway run of *Rent* played for 12 years!

Ryan Steele, Corey Cott, and Jess LeProtto at the Walt Disney World Christmas Parade

Corey Cott

Jack Kelly

I grew up playing sports: basketball, soccer, baseball, golf—you name it, I played it. I also participated in all kinds of clubs, organizations, and events where I was part of a team. Before I was cast in *Newsies*, I felt like I understood and had experienced the meaning of the word "teamwork"—people coming together to accomplish a common goal. Man, I wasn't even close. This show has completely revolutionized the meaning of teamwork for me. From my very first day in the Nederlander Theatre, I felt more welcomed, more included, more essential to a group of people than I did on any number of sports teams. (You can't imagine what our Broadway softball games are like!) This group—the cast, crew, management—is ridiculously special. The bond among all of us is electric, and I truly believe that is why *Newsies* has become a success. Of course, the material is without a doubt brilliant and inspired—but the material can only find truth and life with an exquisite team building it together.

My Broadway debut was August 8, 2012. It was a Wednesday matinee, and besides my wedding day, it was the best day of my life. The show itself was quite a blur, but I remember intermission like it was yesterday. I got to my dressing room after "Santa Fe" and looked at my phone to see almost every cast member had tweeted me "Congrats!" I went up to the ensemble dressing room in tears, almost unable to express how grateful I was for all of these people, who not only welcomed this random new kid to their original cast, but also were encouraging him and supporting him. It was surreal, truly the closest I have felt to actually living in a dream. I guess technically Jack Kelly has the most "solos" and "stage time" or whatever, but here is the truth: all of that DOESN'T MATTA. The show is called *Newsies* not *Jack Kelly: The Musical*, and every morning I wake up just so happy to be a part of the team. Simply as a member. Regardless of what role I play.

LaVon Fisher-Wilson

Here's a *Newsies* secret: when the creative team tells us they are coming to see the show, we totally freak out. No matter how long you've been in the show or how much confidence you have, you still care about what they think. It's like

The cast performing on *Good Morning America*

your parents are in the audience! But Michael Kosarin saying how happy he is with what I've done with the song, Jack Feldman telling me how funny I am, and Alan Menken saying what a wonderful addition I am to the cast just makes my year! And to have a director who trusts you to take adjustments and carry out his vision—Jeff Calhoun is my hero! I'd never met Jeff before my audition, but it felt like we were connected for life after that day.

Adam Kaplan

Morris Delancey

There's something special about the cast of *Newsies*. Maybe it's the material: the strong message of unity and the triumph of an underdog. Or perhaps it's the fact that this show marks many of our Broadway debuts. Regardless of the reason, this company is remarkable. Whenever someone makes their debut (whether in *Newsies* or in a particular role) the company rallies behind them like the newsboys do Jack. Knowing that 30-plus amazing people have your back is indescribable. I was fortunate enough to experience this twice. I made my Broadway debut in *Newsies* on February 19, 2013. I've never been a replacement—that is, I've never had to fill someone else's shoes. But on my opening night I felt like one of the gang. At every entrance or exit, I heard words of encouragement and support. I made a few mistakes here and there, but they didn't matter because I had this fellowship at my side. Surrounded by some of the most talented people in the world and with 20 friends and family members in the audience, I couldn't have asked for a more memorable Broadway debut.

Once I had settled into the show, about a month later, on a morning I made the poor decision to sleep in, I received a call from our stage manager, Thom, letting me know that I would be making my Jack Kelly debut at the matinee. I'll preface this story by saying my put-in rehearsal with the cast for Jack was scheduled for two weeks later. Without any qualms, cast members came to the theater early to help me out in any way possible. I received messages from Jack Feldman, our brilliant lyricist, from Brendon, the other Jack understudy, and Corey—all wishing me luck. Notes, lots of tweets, calls, flowers, you name it—there was no sense of competition or pressure, only a feeling of camaraderie. I had dressers, stagehands, stage managers, and cast members guiding me along, helping me make my principal debut. I'm not the only one who's experienced this feeling of safety and support. The brotherhood that the audience sees onstage is just as present backstage, if not more. We have had many artists join our family since opening, and our swings each cover 14 tracks, so the company has had its fair share of debuts. We are proud to be a part of the show we perform each night. *Newsies* wasn't supposed to come to Broadway; it wasn't supposed to last this long, so it's our job to keep it going and spread the feeling of "one for all, and all for one."

Aaron Albano

We have a lot of Broadway debuts in our cast, especially among the newsies, and to an extent I see them all as my younger brothers. Everyone says that their cast is a family, but ours is different. And watching those guys learn how to be here on Broadway and in a hit show is so wonderful. I admit to being a bit of a "negative Nancy" and telling them not to get used to it—that this is something special and it's not always going to be like this. But at the same time, they are able to teach me how to be excited about it again. If I were with a different show when we did the Macy's Thanksgiving Day Parade, I may have been tempted to act like it wasn't a big deal. But the energy in our cast was so high that I could never have that thought. Jeremy and I talked about this a lot. After a while, you can forget why you're doing this work. So it's nice to remember what it's like to do it for the first time. The best thing about being in *Newsies* with the new guys is that their excitement is genuine, not rehearsed. And even those of us who have done shows before can enjoy what we're doing and remember, "This is what opening night feels like. This is what the Tony Awards feel like." That emotion can still exist.

LaVon Fisher-Wilson

I couldn't do this every night without the full trust that I have in this cast, crew, and creative team. Kara Lindsay and I share a dressing room and instantly became like sisters. Just to hear her say, "You got this!" on days when I'm truly not sure if I got this means the world to me. Kevin Carolan's 20-second improv sessions backstage always kept me laughing. John Dossett wishing me a good show every night and handing me his traditional mints not only lifts my spirits but also freshens my breath! Ever need a hug? Well, just wait until after fight call and several of the newsies will stop by our dressing room and hand them out freely! Our Three Stoogies (Thom, Tim, and Becky) are hands-down the best, and our crew is not only the best but has just as much fun with backstage shenanigans as we do performing the show. My costumes and wigs are to die for, and my dresser Jennie (or Jenquisha) is amazing. And to look down in the orchestra pit and see the shine in conductor Mark Hummel's eyes (and on his head as the light bounces off of it) is all the encouragement I need to wear out my song!

Kara Lindsay

This cast, present and past, are the most wonderful people I know. We don't just come to work, we come to play. My favorite moments are when I am just talking to one of the boys about what's going on in his life. Whether it's difficult, happy, sad, or whatever, I feel happy when they are happy and sad when they are sad. That's how I know they've become my brothers. I would do anything for them. Not to mention my "girlsies." With only five girls in a cast full of boys, you are bound to create a very special bond! (Sometimes you just need to talk about PMS and nail polish.) They literally planned my wedding with me, listening to me blab about every little detail regarding my big day. That's love! Also having the opportunity to share a dressing room with Capathia Jenkins then LaVon Fisher-Wilson allowed me to get to know the two most beautiful women around. *Newsies* has also brought many amazing opportunities . . .

1. Meeting cast members from the *Newsies* movie during the Paper Mill run. So cool to see them supportive of our little show.
2. Performing at the Thanksgiving Day Parade after the Paper Mill run. So early in the morning, but with these boys it doesn't matter what time it is! They were (and are) my Starbucks!
3. Doing our original Broadway cast recording—the first one for many of us!
4. Working together at the Broadway Flea Market.
5. Meeting Bill Pullman, who played the movie character Denton, on which Katherine is partially based. He is one of the many super-cool celebs who came to the show.

The *Newsies* cast with actor Bill Pullman

The World According to Les

Vanessa Brown
child wrangler

Since *Newsies* began Paper Mill rehearsals in August 2011, I have had the great privilege of working with seven incredible young men. They are seven funny, weird, silly, fabulous, smart, and sassy little humans. Each one has brought his own brand of smarts and wit to the part of Les. Vincent Agnello, R.J. Fattori, Matthew Schechter, Lewis Grosso, Jake Lucas, Nick Lampiasi, and Joshua Colley, my life is better for having known you!

Matthew Schechter

About a year before *Newsies* came to Broadway, I was asked to audition for the Paper Mill production. I went to three auditions, after which I heard nothing. I thought my last audition was the "final callback" and I assumed that they were not interested in me. Weeks later, I received a phone call that they wanted to see me the following morning at 10. The only problem was . . . I was on vacation in Hawaii! So the following winter, I was thrilled when the creative team brought me directly to the final callback at Alvin Ailey. I had not been in that building before, and I still pass it and say, "That's where I booked *Newsies*!"

Matthew Schechter at the stage door

Corey Cott with Jake Lucas, Nicholas Lampiasi, and Joshua Colley

Everyone at the show was warm and welcoming and kind. The creative team listened to us, even though we were kids. Lewis and I, who were sharing the role, asked Chris Gattelli if we could dance. He worked with us to see what we could do, then put a little bit in the show for us! Harvey Fierstein, who starred in the first Broadway show I ever saw (*Fiddler on the Roof*), called me Cookie. Being a part of the *Newsies* family, originating the role of Les on Broadway, was a dream come true. In the words of *Mary Poppins* (my other favorite Disney show), anything can happen if you let it.

Lewis Grosso

I first heard about *Newsies* two years ago at a sleepover. We wanted to see an action movie, but my friend's mom said, "What about *Newsies*?" We saw the trailer and liked it, so we watched it. When the auditions came out, I was like, "Oh, I remember that movie. And now it's going to be on Broadway!" For my audition, I had three songs to learn: "Carrying the Banner," part of "King of New York," and "Seize the Day." I was nervous because I really wanted it.

My first Broadway show was *Mary Poppins*, which I did for a year. My last day was February 12, and the first rehearsal for *Newsies* was February 13! I remember eating bagels and Cinnabons. Then I met my wrangler, who was amazing! Her name is Vanessa Brown, and I loved her so much. The first time we got to the Nederlander Theatre, we met the crew and they let us go on the towers. I was with Matthew and we were on the top level—I was almost getting sick. But it was cool because the different levels became different rooms and different places.

When we got to performances, I did the first preview, two times on *Good Morning America* and ABC's *Nightline*. They let Matthew do opening night. Some of the audience knew I was in *Mary Poppins*, so they got to see me on a new stage, in a new show. In *Mary Poppins*, I had to play a snotty rich boy. In *Newsies*, I had to play a dirty poor kid. It was the exact opposite! I was so used to doing a British accent, so I practiced Les's dialogue with my mom. Les was like talking in your regular voice, but I'd still catch myself sometimes starting to talk like Michael Banks!

The Tony Awards were amazing. When I was younger, my mom and my sister and I would always watch it together. My dad wouldn't be very interested. I would watch the shows and their acts and I thought that was so cool. I sometimes wished that I could be on it. And then I ended up doing it! It was amazing to be in front of the crowd and to know that I was on TV. It's something that I can't even explain. It's so nerve-wracking and so exciting. And then we got to see Christopher get his award for Best Choreography. That was cool. We were all screaming at the TV and congratulating him and calling him up.

One of the best parts of *Newsies* was that I was never treated like a little boy that they couldn't be around and act normal with. Some guys would take me out to dinner, or we'd go to someone's apartment. Aaron Albano was awesome. I always wanted a dog and he has a beagle. He let me come to his apartment in Queens so I could hang out with the dog. Turns out that I might be getting a dog for my sixth-grade graduation. I want a Lakeland terrier.

Jake Lucas

Being on a Broadway stage with amazingly talented folks and in front of a live audience is more than I ever expected to be doing at 10 years old. It was the chance of a lifetime, and I feel that I've won the lottery to get to be part of the *Newsies* family forever! Here's a list of my favorite memories during my six months in *Newsies*:

1. Broadway debut on 9/10/2012 with the twins, Jacob and David Guzman. First-ever twins on Broadway, right?
2. Extraordinary wrangler, Vanessa (and backups Rachel, Bobby, and Thomas), and loving dresser, Jenny.
3. Those special moments chatting with or getting encouragement from the Disney creative team and staff and, of course, the daily greetings from the Nederlander staff.
4. My sister, Sydney, and I getting to bond with Nick (the other Les), and all the times hanging out between shows, dancing in the Nederlander hallway, or dreaming up our next technology adventure. Lifelong friends!

Jake Lucas

5. Gypsy of the Year rehearsal and performance with Vanessa and Kevin as writers and JP Ferreri as choreographer.

6. Meeting all of the celebrities who saw Nick or me perform.

7. Learning how to knit from Rachel and making Kara Lindsay a headband for her birthday.

8. Sending Ryan Steele on an amazing Secret Santa scavenger hunt with hilarious video taken along the way (and watching Ryan do any dance move).

9. Wailing on the high notes and harmonizing with Kara, Corey, and Ben in "Watch What Happens."

10. Learning the "King of New York" tap steps from Michael Fatica, the Guzman twins, Mike Faist (the nerve tap, yeah!), Garett Hawe, Julian DeGuzman, and Jack Scott.

11. Playing board games and talking with the girlsies. Girlsie hugs are the best!

12. Brady's antics and conversations, and John Dossett and Kevin Carolan being so sweet to me.

13. Stage managers Thom and Becky always being nice, and Tim always playing games.

14. Cool conversations and darts with Eduardo.

15. Getting to sing in the Disney interview with Tim Federle—definitely a highlight that opened other doors!

16. Being in the *Newsies* commercial! I get so excited every time I see it.

17. The Oscars party with Jeff Calhoun and the *Newsies* first anniversary party, where I got to see Jeremy Jordan again since meeting him at my very first fight call.

18. Stage hugs from Medda (LaVon) and Katherine (Kara)—always something I looked forward to.

19. Having my hand go numb signing posters and Playbills during the pizza parties while being surrounded by great *Newsies* friends.

20. Getting kisses, gum, cookies, newsletters, cards, etc. from the ever-supportive and loyal Fansies.

Joshua Colley

I'm 11 years old and this is my first Broadway show. It's been amazing to go up there every night and perform with all these talented people in the cast. My favorite part is being able to sing all that beautiful music. I am always looking up to Alan Menken because he's written *Aladdin* and *Tangled* and *Beauty and the Beast*. I watched those as a kid. Well, I'm still a kid. I only heard about *Newsies* when my mom said that I was going to audition for it. I didn't see the movie before I auditioned, and I still haven't seen it to this day! But I thought it was really cool when I found out it was about a newspaper strike.

When I went into the audition, I thought, "Okay, I'm gonna get this." I had practiced all the songs and I thought I had the lines perfectly. But when I got up there, I was just like, "Ummmmm. What's the next line?" I forgot the lines, but they were totally chill about it. They gave me the sides, I read the lines, and then went to the airport. I was in *Les Miz* at the time, so I was about to fly back, and in the morning my dad was going to fly to Tampa, where my mom and brother were still on vacation. My dad was scrolling through his voice mails and found my agent's number. He listened to it and did a thumbs up. I was like, "Yes! I got the part." I felt like I had to tell someone. So when we got on the plane, I told the flight attendant everything that happened.

Being a replacement was different but still wonderful. The cast made me feel like I'd been there for ages and was their best friend. I would do the show as I was told and then the stage manager would come in and give me notes. Sometimes the notes were the same, sometimes they were different. I take direction very well, so mostly they were different. My favorite part of the show is the reprise of "Watch What Happens," because it goes through all the different stages of acting—from funny to dramatic to sad, to all these different things.

I've been acting a really long time. My mom and dad own a children's theater company. They were doing shows and I thought, "Wow, that's really cool. I should try that." I was about eight when I did *A Christmas Carol*. I did some school shows before that, but that was my first professional show and really fun. I want to keep acting as I get older. I think of it as a passion. My advice to other kids who want to perform is: never give up. If you want something, you should keep striving to get it. Performing is an amazing experience and I think other people should try it.

OPPOSITE: Lewis Grosso and Matthew Schechter with Luke Edwards, the original Les from the film.

them, and

FANSIES

Marissa Scarangella, St. John's, FL

FANSIES

Cassidy Shuflin, Midway, UT

Julia Simoes de Oliveira, Sao Pa

"My seven-year-old son didn't move once during the entire performance. He was so moved that we bought him a souvenir hat, and he didn't take it off the rest of the day. When we returned home, he slung a knapsack across his back and stuck the souvenir paper inside it. He made $7 off my husband and me just reselling the same paper. *Newsies* was also my five-year-old daughter's first Broadway show. She now listens to "Watch What Happens" over and over again. *Newsies* provided our fabulous family of four with one of our best days together."

— Mindy Heimbach, Nazareth, PA

FANSIES

Marisa Pittarelli, Park Ridge, NJ

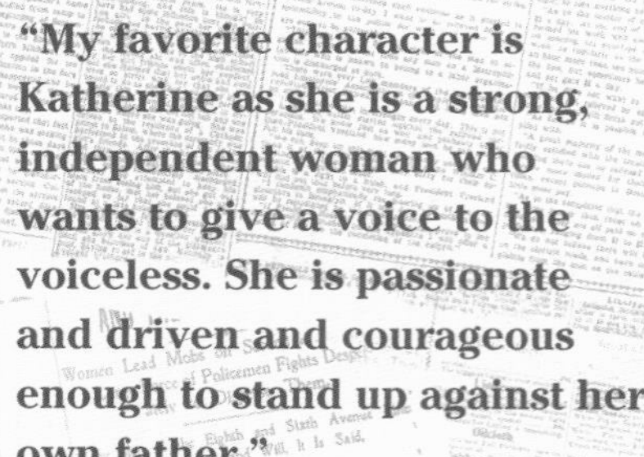

"My favorite character is Katherine as she is a strong, independent woman who wants to give a voice to the voiceless. She is passionate and driven and courageous enough to stand up against her own father."

— Grace Delmar, Keller, TX

FANSIES

Nate Patrick Siebert, Denver, CO

"I saw it in July 2012 when I was seven. When I'm 10, I'm going to be Les on Broadway."

— Nate Patrick Siebert, Denver, CO

FANSIES

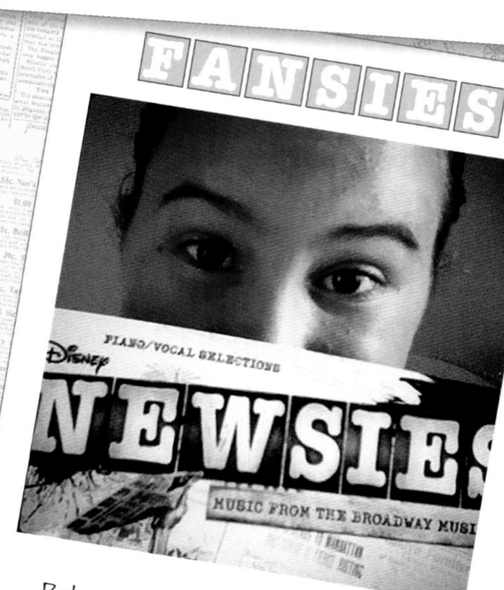

Rebecca Bailey, Newport Beach, CA

"After seeing *Newsies*, it made me realize how much fun it would be to be a dancer in a big Broadway production. I have been taking dance classes for a while now, and my dream is to one day make it to Broadway. I look up to every single one of the cast members. They are all my role models."

— Kayla Gmoser, Churchville, PA

Lindsey Halwachs, Seattle, WA

Erica Redmond, Penrose, CO

"*Newsies* reminds me of the time our school board tried to cut music classics at the high school. We refused to step down and let that happen. We all went to a board meeting wearing shirts from our bands, orchestra, choir, and drama club. And because we fought so hard for what we believed in, we got to keep almost everything. This spring, our class came to see *Newsies* and we were reminded of how hard we fought to get the education we wanted and deserved."

— Janna Kozloski, South Glen Falls, NY

Emily Hornburg, Chicago, IL

Tommy Faircloth, Columbia, SC

"Opening a handwritten letter from Corey Cott made me feel like he knew me. They seem to actually care about their fans, and that doesn't happen in many other places."

— Olivia Thompson, Beavercreek, OH

Marissa Casano, Troy, MI

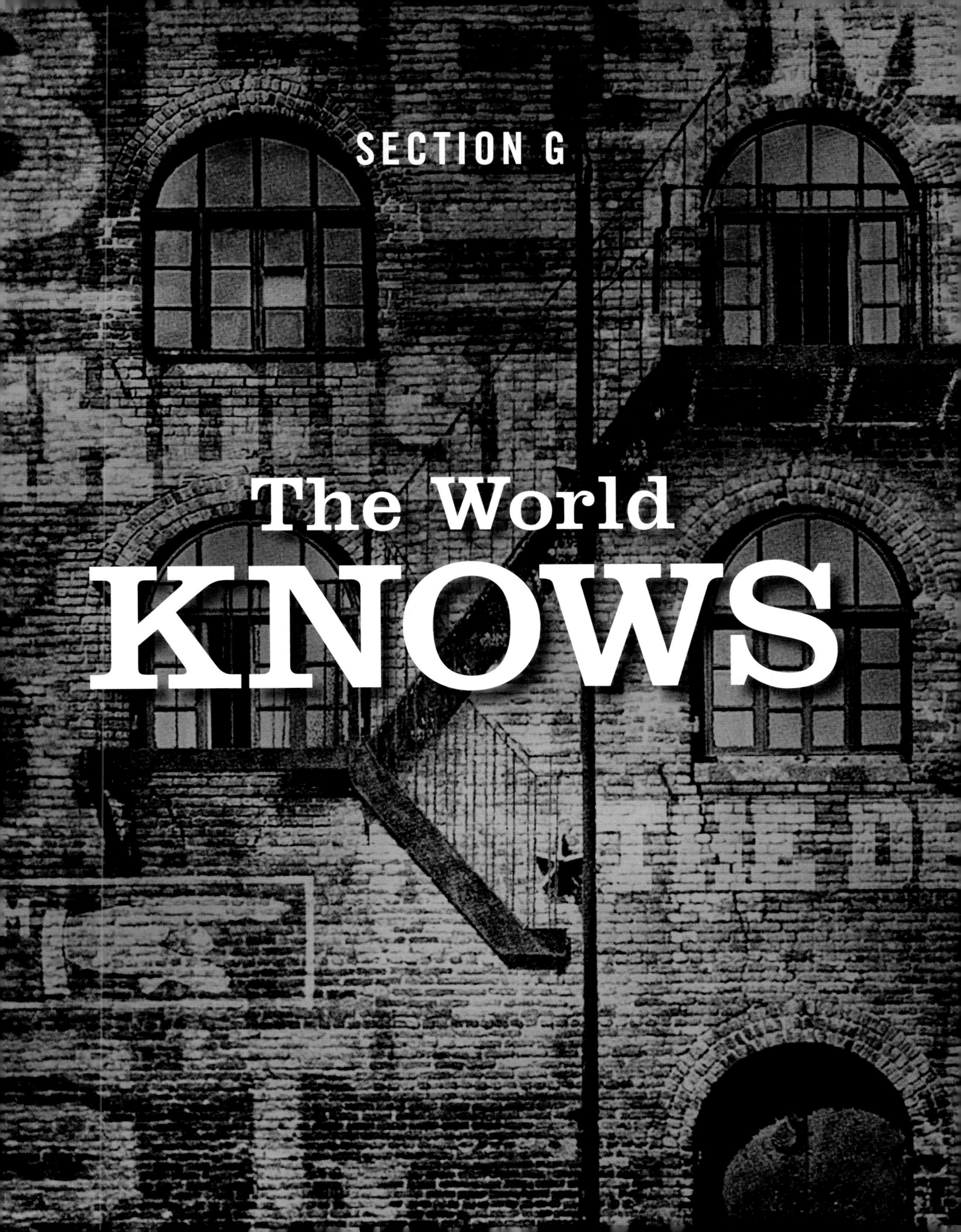

SECTION G

The World KNOWS

Final Reflections from the *Newsies* Family

Harvey Fierstein

In the end, Alan, Jack, and I came up with a version of the show that excited Mr. Schumacher enough that he mounted a production at Paper Mill Playhouse. And that production was received so well that we brought it to New York City for a limited engagement. And that went so well that we won a whole mess of awards, and the show is already in its second year at the Nederlander Theatre on Broadway. And, one day, it will be provided to schools, colleges, and theaters around the world for productions, just as planned. This really was a story with a classic Disney happy ending. BUT (why is there always a but?) the real joy for me was working with Alan and Jack. From our first meeting in 2009 to the opening night on Broadway in 2012, the three of us joked and laughed and played together like the three happiest kids in the playground. The only thing more joyous is the heartwarming thrill we feel whenever we stand in the back of the theater and watch audiences become infected with the exuberance that is *Newsies*, the Tony Award–winning musical. So, the moral of my tale? You can't celebrate the victory if you don't take the challenge.

Michael Cohen

publicity director, DTG

My first internship while attending Ithaca College was with Walt Disney Pictures Publicity in New York City in 1992. The first movie I worked on was *Newsies*. I remember sitting in the theater, resonating with every moment, and thinking, "This needs to be a Broadway musical." Over the years, like many others, I watched *Newsies* on VHS, then DVD—still thinking, "Why hasn't Disney made this into a Broadway musical?" It was my first day working at DTG in 2010 when I found out that *Newsies* was being produced at Paper Mill Playhouse. It was fate—a full-circle moment. Now that we've passed its first year on Broadway, I relish that I was part of this unlikely and successful journey. Working in publicity and being part of all the great and unique stories we've been able to execute continues to be a labor of love. In 1899, the newsies of New York used the technology of their time, the printing press, for their voices to be heard. Today, we get to use the vast technology of the 21st century in TV, radio, print, and online social media to allow our voices to be heard and to help tell this great story about the show we call *Newsies*.

Jeff Calhoun

Given all the joy, love, respect, and admiration among everyone involved with the creation of *Newsies*, our success with audiences can be summed up in a word . . . heart.

Ricky Hinds

associate director

When I was 11 years old, I saw the movie *Newsies* for the first time . . . and it changed my life. I had been dancing for about six years and already knew musical theater was what I was going to do when I grew up. But it wasn't until I saw those newsboys dancing their hearts out that I realized it was okay to be a boy in the performing arts. Almost 18 years later, I was sitting at Jeff Calhoun's apartment when he mentioned that Disney was interested in having him direct a stage production of *Newsies*. I nearly fell out of my seat! I began singing some of the songs to him, and although I guarantee you I did no justice to Alan Menken's amazing score, Jeff and I soon began our journey with the show together. I was beyond thrilled to make my Broadway debut as the associate director. This show has bettered my life in many ways and its message speaks to everyone. Seize the day!

Myriah Perkins

production manager, DTG

What was so remarkable about the *Newsies* experience was that the story we were telling onstage was being echoed offstage in what we were trying to accomplish with the show itself. Sitting in tech, I was struck by the lyrics of Katherine's song as she prepares to write her first article covering the newsies' strike: "We're doing something no one's even tried, and, yes, we're terrified, but watch what happens." Behind the scenes, there we were, breaking the mold of the historically big Disney musicals and about to put *Newsies* out in front of the world. The mixed emotions of fear and excitement were palpable. As a longtime fan of the movie, I desperately wanted the show to be the success I knew it could be, but how would audiences and critics react? Time would soon tell for this little show that could, and now, the rest of the world... will know!

John Dossett

As you get older, you appreciate things more—and all the work and luck and craft and commitment that goes into them. There is nothing like being in a big, fat Broadway hit. Nothing. It's something you dream about being a part of, made all the sweeter because you are the creators of these characters. I am the villain of *Newsies*. And I am loving every second of it. Every second. We once had a Tuesday matinee, largely composed of school groups. They were a terrific audience, attentive and participatory. As I took my bow at curtain call, I was greeted with a chorus of boos. It was some of the sweetest music I have ever heard. I take great pride and joy in saying I am the actual cannibal Joseph Pulitzer.

Aaron Albano

Being in *Newsies* surpassed all of my expectations. I have always been one of those guys who has never cried after shows. When we closed Paper Mill, we didn't know we were going to Broadway. And there are pictures to prove it—I was a mess. Eduardo gave us a "Newsies Banner" of our whole story. At that time, I thought, "I'll never sing these songs again." I was a bad storyteller that day, because I was a wreck. It meant too much to me. With this group of guys, this creative team, it was kismet. Beforehand, I thought it was going to be a good show. And I've been part of good shows before. This really became something else. It has redefined my expectations. At talkbacks, people ask me, "What's your favorite show?" And it sounds cheesy, but it's the one I'm doing.

Lauren Daghini

marketing brand manager, DTG

Working on *Newsies* reminded me why I'm in this business to begin with. There was an energy in this building that was a little intoxicating. We knew we were working really hard for something that we all believed in and were desperately rooting for it to succeed. And that was exciting. I remember sitting in the audience the night of the final dress and being incredibly proud to be a part of what was happening in that theater, knowing it was something special.

Andy Richardson

My *Newsies* journey has been incredible. I got to originate the role of Romeo, a character not in the movie but created for the stage production. I've performed in the Macy's Thanksgiving Day Parade, on *The View*, on *Good Morning America*, and on the Tony Awards. I'm on the original Broadway cast recording. Now, I'm Crutchie. After understudying the character for a year, this is my first principal role. More importantly, I've made friends that I'll have forever. My coworkers are my family. They make me look forward to going to work each day. People ask if I get tired of doing *Newsies* eight times a week after so long. I always laugh at the mere thought of that. I could do this show for 20 years and still never get tired of hearing that trumpet start the overture, laughing onstage with my friends and brothers, singing the lyrics that still give me chills. I will always love this show and be grateful to be a part of the *Newsies* family.

Mark Hoebee

Newsies being such a success is huge for us. In Paper Mill's 75-year history, *Newsies* is the first original musical to premiere here and then move to Broadway. So it is something that everybody—staff, board, donors, and the foundations who support us—feels excited about. I am thrilled! People tell me all the time, "Well, Disney knew they were going to move it to New York." And I say, "No, that's not true!" It was a result of all the best things: an incredible group of creatives, producers, and partners working to get the best show together that we possibly could. That is what happened. And the result was so good that it naturally made the move. It wasn't one of those pre-planned, "we're going to force it, we're going to make it happen" things. We couldn't be more honored to be a part of *Newsies* and to be associated with Disney. It's just amazing for us at Paper Mill and for me personally.

Michael Fatica

Newsies still gives me the same feeling now as when I watched the movie as a wee little guy. Being a newsie is a gift to any actor, both on- and offstage. If my seventh-grade self could have seen into the future, he would have warned himself about many things, namely the haircut I had in 2007, but he would have been honored and proud to know that that seventh-grade performance wouldn't be his last in a newsie cap. Newsies forever, boys. (And girls. And oldsies.)

Ryan Steele

Specs, dance captain

I didn't completely understand what I was getting myself into when I signed my contract for *Newsies*. I knew I would be working with some of the most talented performers of our generation. I knew I'd be singing songs that I've loved my whole life. I also knew I'd be working with one of the most brilliant choreographers I've ever met. I did not know that the talented young performers would soon become my best friends, whom I'm sure will be in my life forever. I also didn't know that I would be recording some of my favorite songs on an original Broadway cast recording. And I definitely didn't know that I would be brought to tears watching our fearless leader win a Tony Award for the choreography that I was lucky enough to dance eight times a week. Above all, I didn't know I was signing up for a life-changing experience. The feeling I got every time I walked into the Nederlander Theatre was family. The entire company shared something very special: a deep love for our show. It's very rare that everyone on a team is equally as passionate about the project that they are working on. I was lucky enough to experience universal passion at *Newsies*. I can't even begin to explain how grateful I am. When I left the show in January 2013, I took with me countless memories that I will look back on with pride and nostalgia. I'm excited to see where the show goes and the lives it will touch in the future. Newsies forever!

Colleen McCormack

A few weeks after I started working at Disney Theatrical Group, our licensing department was toying with the idea of creating a small stage version of *Newsies* for high schools and community theaters. It was slow going and no one thought very much of the show until we had our first reading in May 2010. The show wasn't quite done, but it was thrilling to hear Alan Menken and Jack Feldman's glorious score and see what *Newsies* might be like onstage. From that first reading, it was as if a boulder had been pushed down a hill. Little by little, the show got better and better and all of a sudden, we were beginning a pilot production at the Paper Mill Playhouse. And right around opening night of Paper Mill, I found out I was pregnant with my first child. The rest is history—the review in *The New York Times*, the performances on *The View* and at Macy's Thanksgiving Day Parade, and the announcement of the transfer. I was seven months pregnant by the time we started previews on Broadway, and my department continually joked that my daughter would be organizing strikes in day care from hearing the score too many times. But as I sat putting together the vocal selections book of the Broadway score, I couldn't help welling up with tears. I truly hope that *Newsies* is still running when she's old enough to see it—or at least stage a performance in our living room!

Ryan Breslin

Race

I have to give the Fansies my endless gratitude for making this show what it is. Y'all are hilarious, creative, good-hearted, and unconditional to us newsies. We're so spoiled. This experience is hard to put into words. I'm about to turn 24 and I began my journey with *Newsies* at age 21. It's been like a second college experience, but this time I got to be in a sort of musical-theater frat house, brah. My favorite experiences with this group have to be the ridiculous hours spent preparing a press event. When these boys get jet-lagged, I turn into a 12-year-old boy who thinks anything and everything is funny. This group already makes me laugh, but slap-happy newsies are one-of-a-kind wieners who can't be replaced by anyone. We're so lucky to be a part of a cast that not only gets along, but also are great friends outside of the theater.

Luke Camp

merchandise team, DTG

This show is one of the most invigorating, inspiring, and energetic musicals on Broadway today! At the end of every performance, eight times a week, the entire theater shakes with the cheers of the 1,207 audience members, and it reminds me how incredible this art form is.

Julie Foldesi

ensemble

Newsies has been beyond a joyful experience. I have worked with some of the most amazing people I've ever worked with in my career. We also had such an exciting journey. I did one of the readings of *Newsies*, and it was clear that this piece was a winner. Not long after, I was cast in the Paper Mill production, which was a delightful rehearsal process and then a thrilling ride as we watched the throngs of fans come and devote their hearts to this show. Then there was promise of the Macy's Thanksgiving Day

Parade, but no definite word about a future. And not long after that we were headed to the Nederlander for multiple standing ovations during our first shows there. The joy in the audience and the joy shared with the family we created while telling this incredible story were special. There were also some special people we had to leave behind—like Mrs. Baum, Davey and Les's mother, whom I played at Paper Mill, and Patrick's mother, the character from the movie that we as a company fought to put back in the show for the Broadway run (it seemed a true possibility for a second). They were decent ladies, fighting to help their children in difficult times.

Kara Lindsay

To me, *Newsies* has meant family, home, and dreams come true. I made my Broadway debut alongside the greatest group of brothers and sisters I could ever ask for. Many of them were making their debuts as well, which made it all the more special. Every single part of this *Newsies* journey has been truly remarkable: from Paper Mill to Macy's Thanksgiving Day Parade to a Broadway run to the unbelievable support of the Fansies to the Tonys to our one-year anniversary!

Thom Gates

This show is special for me in many ways. Although I didn't sell newspapers on the street, I was a paperboy from the age of 12 till I was 17, delivering the "papes" to about 80 households in a small town in upstate New York where newspaper reading was voracious at the time. With that job and a few others in school, I raised enough money for the first few years of college. The inner paperboy in me still sometimes comes out, and I'm proud to be "Carrying the Banner" each day. I've been blessed to have worked on a show with such a dedicated team of cast members and creative staff who really care about the show and what happens on a daily basis.

Tommy Bracco

Spot Conlon

How could I possibly put this experience into words?! This show has completely changed my life. *Newsies* gave me the courage to do things I never thought I could. It's about fighting hard for what you believe in, and that's what we do every night. My favorite part is how much the show reflects real life. The newsies are a family in the show, and that's exactly what the actors who play them are—one big, loud, crazy family (and that's coming from an Italian, so you know it must be true). When the newsies make the front page of the pape, they make history. We are making musical theater history here! We are dancing our butts off eight times a week at the Nederlander and on national television, inspiring people from all over the world. It's not just about us and the fun we're having. It's about the 1,200 people in the audience every show. It's about that little boy sitting in the front row with his newsie cap on. It's about the girls jumping up to try and catch the papers we throw in "Seize the Day." It's about the people who give standing ovations in the middle of the show and who continue to come back over and over. Thank you. All of our dreams have come true because of you.

Andrew Hollenbeck

sales assistant, DTG

When *Newsies* began at Paper Mill Playhouse, I was working for Dragonflyer Works Inc., the flyering company DTG uses at TKTS. As a huge Disney fan, I knew I had to see this show, so I entered the ticket raffle for free tickets to the final dress rehearsal. It absolutely blew me away and I knew that this show would have a bigger life. Once *Newsies* announced a Broadway run, Dragonflyer was asked to take on the lottery for a limited number of $30 tickets to every performance. The opening-night lottery was one of the coolest experiences I've ever had—there were well over 300 people who were dying to see the show, and you could tell right away that *Newsies* was going to be a hit. The lottery crowds at the Nederlander Theatre grew and were full of people of all ages. We had little matinee ladies who would play the lotto 12 times until they finally won. We had teenaged "Fansies" who had seen the show 15 times already and were back for more. We had families from out of town with children dressed in full *Newsies* costumes. Audiences' dedication to the show is amazing. As *Newsies*' success has continued, so has mine—I landed a part-time job with Disney Theatrical as the press clerk, and now I work full-time in the sales office. I am so proud to continue to be a part of this incredible Broadway show!

Stuart Zagnit

We live in a world that is like "Look at me, look at me!" But the best stuff doesn't scream at you. It just says "I am here." You don't see the wheels turning. *Newsies* is based on a historical event, but it is not a sentimental show. Jeff took great pains to avoid that in casting. Jeremy set a tone that was great, and Corey continues that now. People like Ryan Breslin—he's not sentimental, but he is such a perfect character and he looks like he has been pulled right out of another century. There is nobody on the planet that looks like him! That uniqueness of character and the lack of sentimentality give a harder edge that I think people relate to as historical event rather than a cartoony representation of it. And when you get to the dancing, it is celebratory, but it is also mature, and it's phenomenal. I don't know how many hundreds of times I've seen certain numbers, but I don't get tired of watching them. The newsies give it their all every night. It is just wonderful to see. And it's helped by the enthusiasm we get from the crowds. I never cease to be amazed by it.

J. Allen Suddeth

Did I ever think that working in New Jersey, with a young cast, for a director I'd never met, on a set 30 feet high, on a show I'd never heard of, and for a famous producing organization who'd never heard of me would pay off, go to Broadway, and last over a year? No way!

LaVon Fisher-Wilson

I love telling the story of *Newsies* six days a week, mainly because the underdogs win, and that's what I have always considered myself to be. I wasn't the kid who got picked to succeed in my performing-arts high school. As a matter a fact, I remember singing a solo in a musical in front of the stage curtain while bullies stood behind the curtain and taunted me. But I didn't give up, and look at me now—I'm in *Newsies*. Yes, it does get better! What we sing about every night is true. If you fight for what you believe in, you can make a difference, and that is exactly what we do on that stage: we make people believe in dreams again. That is what *Newsies* has done for me.

Chris Montan

What is so gratifying all these years later is that this music we really believed in turned out to be something that audiences believe in, too.

Jeff Croiter

Newsies is now my longest-running Broadway show. A year later, of course there are things that I would do slightly differently, or alterations or additions I would make to cueing. But I don't think anything I do to the show as a lighting designer would make the audience enjoy it any more than they already are. People love the show and that's all that matters!

Jeff Lee

Last year we did a revue of Disney's theatrical songs on a cruise, and the encore was from *Newsies*. As the emcee I asked the audience, "Does anybody know a new Disney show running right now on Broadway that we didn't even talk about a few years ago?" I thought it was going to be two or three people, then a bunch going, "Huh?" It wasn't! There was an overwhelming response to *Newsies*. Ironic that it was probably one of the least successful films Disney ever made and now it is one of the most successful shows that we have put on the stage. The score is thrilling. Even the songs that got cut or replaced—I think they were all great. It was just a matter of constantly going for something better. I just love the score, every time I hear it. It's got energy, it's got youth, it's got passion. I think it's fantastic.

Alex Wong

Newsies was an absolute dream come true. I knew I was going to like it a lot, but I didn't know that I was going to LOVE it. It has become one of my proudest accomplishments and I hold it so close to my heart. At my last show, I broke out into tears during the bows because I couldn't believe that this chapter was over. It seemed too soon, but as they say, once a newsie, always a newsie! Newsies forever!

Justin Huff

From the first preview of *Newsies* at Paper Mill Playhouse to its current Broadway run at the Nederlander, I have stood in the back of both theaters many times, always with a big smile on my face. As I watch our cast perform the very songs that inspired me as a child, I am reminded that you can achieve any dream you put your mind to. And it's that message that I hope will continue to inspire generations of young boys to chase their dreams.

Corey Cott

I just want to express how much gratitude I have for every person who makes this show happen. Thank you to every crew member, every cast member, every ticket taker, every concessions worker for contributing to this experience and literally making dreams come true. You inspire me, move me, and lift me higher than I ever thought I could go. I love each and every one of you so much.

LaVon Fisher-Wilson

The Fansies are a mighty, mighty group. When I started a *Newsies* trivia game on my fan page, I got over 100 posts in 24 hours. I had to take a pause, 'cause I had no idea what I was dealing with! These are kids who were moved after watching the movie, and they carry the banner with us every day all around the world. They know the songs, the history . . . honey, they even schooled me! They are truly our voices across the globe and we wouldn't be here without them.

Mark Hummel

Sometimes when you're offered things, you don't necessarily want to do them eight times a week. But I like doing *Newsies* eight times a week. It's fun, it's a good score, and it's a true story. And Alan Menken got his Tony Award! I was so proud to be part of that, knowing him for so long. He gets a prize on the one that I was conducting. And Chris Gattelli got a Tony Award for his choreography as well. I thought, "I helped him with that." It was so validating.

Christopher Gattelli

I think what draws people to *Newsies* is that it's the classic case of the underdog. There isn't a single person who hasn't felt like an outsider or that they're not given their due. The special thing about the show is that you have this young group of newsies who work incredibly hard and are not appreciated for their work, much less given credit for it. They then band together and this phenomenal thing happens: they actually *do* make a difference in the world. And that same thing is happening live for the audience. Our boys on stage are young guys who are working hard and trying to make a difference. They come together every night, they do something phenomenal, and they're changing the world. To have it play out in real time every night as you're watching these young men do what they do is genuine magic. You can't get that anywhere else.

Eduardo Castro

The cast was asked to perform in the opening number of the 2013 Tony Awards at Radio City Music Hall. Right before we went live, we were in the back of the house ready for our entrance, and all of a sudden, we just went into a huddle. It was all of the newsies, Thom Gates, Rick Kelly and Keith Shaw from wardrobe, and me. We get in a huddle in the back of auditorium with tons of people walking around us—the camera crews, the security, the ushers. And I think it was Corey Cott who said, "I just need to let you guys know that this means so much for me to be here. It is truly a dream to be able to be on the Tony Awards." And everybody starts crying. I'm looking around the faces of these guys and everyone is so emotional—Julian DeGuzman is crying, Brendon Stimson can't look at me—and there is that sense of energy and gratitude and excitement. Nothing is taken for granted. It is so amazing that even a year later, to have that moment right before you go live, right before you go onstage, to have that opportunity to be thankful. I keep telling them, "You have to take it in, every moment. You never take it for granted. We were given 12 weeks, and look where we are now. As with everything in life, you never know when it will go away. So you have to live for the moment and you have to be grateful that you are the one who gets the chance to do this, because there are so many other kids and performers and people who would love to be in your shoes." That night was such a validation of what this show is and the passion that is still so alive in the theater.

Noni White

I envisioned success against all probability, trusting that it would come at the right time. We do what we do not only to entertain but also to provoke—to make people think, laugh, and cry. I feel blessed every day that I do something I love. I envision a long life for *Newsies* on Broadway and beyond. The play has touched many people, touched different generations, and I trust it will touch countless more for years to come. I will be forever grateful to the real-life newsies, whose courage inspired us all; to the fans who drove *Newsies*' success; and to Steve Fickinger and Tom Schumacher for being great shepherds. Without Tom's enthusiasm, support, and blessing, this never would have happened.

The Broadway Company of *Newsies*, July 23, 2012

EXTRA!
NEWSIES SETS AND BREAKS SEVEN
NEDERLANDER THEATRE BOX-OFFICE RECORDS!!!
HELL'S
KITCHEN
NEW YORK CITY

Opening Night, March 29, 2012

Disney Theatrical Productions
under the direction of
Thomas Schumacher

Presents

Music by
ALAN MENKEN

Lyrics by
JACK FELDMAN

Book by
HARVEY FIERSTEIN

Based on the Disney film written by BOB TZUDIKER and NONI WHITE

Starring
JEREMY JORDAN

JOHN DOSSETT KARA LINDSAY CAPATHIA JENKINS BEN FANKHAUSER
ANDREW KEENAN-BOLGER LEWIS GROSSO MATTHEW SCHECHTER

AARON J. ALBANO MARK ALDRICH TOMMY BRACCO JOHN E. BRADY RYAN BRESLIN
KEVIN CAROLAN CAITLYN CAUGHELL KYLE COFFMAN MIKE FAIST MICHAEL FATICA
JULIE FOLDESI GARETT HAWE THAYNE JASPERSON EVAN KASPRZAK JESS LEPROTTO
STUART MARLAND ANDY RICHARDSON JACK SCOTT RYAN STEELE BRENDON STIMSON
NICK SULLIVAN EPHRAIM SYKES LAURIE VELDHEER ALEX WONG STUART ZAGNIT

Scenic Design
TOBIN OST

Costume Design
JESS GOLDSTEIN

Lighting Design
JEFF CROITER

Sound Design
KEN TRAVIS

Projection & Video Design
SVEN ORTEL

Hair & Wig Design
CHARLES G. LAPOINTE

Fight Direction
J. ALLEN SUDDETH

Casting
TELSEY + COMPANY

Associate Producer
ANNE QUART

Technical Supervision
NEIL MAZZELLA & GEOFF QUART

Production Manager
EDUARDO CASTRO

Production Stage Manager
THOMAS J. GATES

Music Director/ Dance Music Arrangements
MARK HUMMEL

Music Coordinator
JOHN MILLER

Associate Director
RICHARD J. HINDS

Associate Choreographer
LOU CASTRO

Orchestrations by
DANNY TROOB

Music Supervision/ Incidental Music & Vocal Arrangements by
MICHAEL KOSARIN

Choreographed by
CHRISTOPHER GATTELLI

Directed by
JEFF CALHOUN

World Premiere, Paper Mill Playhouse, in Millburn, New Jersey on September 25, 2011. Mark S. Hoebee, Producing Artistic Director, Todd Schmidt, Managing Director

Newsies Cast Members through First Anniversary on Broadway

Aaron J. Albano – Finch, Ensemble
Mark Aldrich – Seitz, Ensemble
Vincent Agnello – Les (Paper Mill)
Helen Anker – Medda Larkin, Ensemble (Paper Mill)
Tommy Bracco* – Spot Conlon, Scab, Ensemble
John E. Brady – Wiesel, Stage Manager, Mr. Jacobi, Mayor, Ensemble
Ryan Breslin* – Race, Ensemble
Kevin Carolan – Roosevelt, Nunzio, Ensemble
Caitlyn Caughell* – Swing
Kyle Coffman – Henry, Ensemble
Joshua Colley* – Les
Corey Cott* – Jack Kelly
Julian DeGuzman* – Swing
John Dossett – Joseph Pulitzer
Max Ehrich – Mush, Darcy, Ensemble (Paper Mill)
Mike Faist* – Morris Delancy, Ensemble
Ben Fankhauser* – Davey
Michael Fatica* – Swing
RJ Fattori – Les (Paper Mill)
JP Ferreri* – Buttons, Swing
LaVon Fisher-Wilson – Medda Larkin
John Michael Fiumara* – Specs, Ensemble
Julie Foldesi – Nun, Ensemble
Hogan Fulton* – Darcy, Ensemble
Lewis Grosso – Les
David Guzman* – Mush, Ensemble
Jacob Guzman* – Sniper, Scab, Ensemble
Garett Hawe – Albert, Bill, Ensemble
Liana Hunt – Hannah, Nun, Ensemble
Corey Hummerston – Bill, Ensemble (Paper Mill)
Thayne Jasperson* – Darcy, Ensemble
Capathia Jenkins – Medda Larkin
Jeremy Jordan – Jack Kelly
Adam Kaplan* – Morris Delancey, Ensemble
Evan Kasprzak* – Elmer, Ensemble
Andrew Keenan-Bolger – Crutchie
Nicholas Lampiasi* – Les
Jess LeProtto – Buttons, Scab, Ensemble
Kara Lindsay* – Katherine
Jake Lucas* – Les
Stuart Marland – Snyder, Ensemble
Tommy Martinez* – Romeo, Ensemble
Michael McArthur – Swing (Paper Mill)
Ron Raines – Joseph Pulitzer
Andy Richardson – Romeo, Crutchie
Tom Alan Robbins – Roosevelt, Nunzio, Ensemble
Matthew Schechter – Les
Jack Scott* – Swing
Scott Shedenhelm – Sniper, Ensemble (Paper Mill)
Ryan Steele – Specs, Ensemble
Brendon Stimson – Oscar Delancey, Ensemble
Nick Sullivan – Bunsen, Ensemble
Ephraim Sykes – Mush, Ensemble
Clay Thomson* – Spot Conlon, Scab, Ensemble
Madeline Trumble* – Katherine Standby
Laurie Veldheer* – Hannah, Nun, Ensemble
Alex Wong* – Sniper, Scab, Ensemble
Iain Young* – Henry, Ensemble
Stuart Zagnit – Swing

* *Broadway debut*

Newsies Staff, Opening Night, March 29, 2012

COMPANY MANAGER........EDUARDO CASTRO
Production Stage Manager........Thomas J. Gates
Assistant Company Manager........Emily Powell
Stage Manager........Timothy Eaker
Assistant Stage Manager........Becky Fleming
Production Coordinator........Kerry McGrath
Dance Captain........Ryan Steele
Assistant Dance Captain........Michael Fatica
Fight Captain........Kevin Carolan
Production Assistants........Bryan Bradford,
........Patrick Egan,
........Aaron Elgart,
........Mark A.Stys,
........Amanda Tamny

DISNEY ON BROADWAY PUBLICITY
Senior Publicist........Dennis Crowley
Associate Publicist........Michelle Bergmann

Associate Scenic Designer........Christine Peters
Assistant Scenic Designer........Jerome Martin
Assistant Set Designer........John Raley
Associate Costume Designer........Mike Floyd
Associate Costume Designer........China Lee
Associate Lighting Designer........Cory Pattak
Assistant Lighting Designer........Wilburn Bonnell
Associate Sound Designer........Alexander Hawthorne
Moving Light Programmer........Victor Seastone
Assistant Projection Designer........Lucy Mackinnon
Assistant to the Projection Designer........Gabes Rives-Corbett
Projection Programmer........Florian Mosleh
Assistant Hair and Wig Designer........Leah Loukas
Assistant Fight Director........Ted Sharon
Technical Supervisor........Neil Mazzella
Technical Direction........Troika Entertainment
Technical Associates........Irene Wang, Sam Ellis
Technical Production Assistant........Canara Price
Advance Carpenter........Sam Mahan
Head Carpenter........Eddie Bash
Automation........Karl Schuberth
Carpenter........Michael Allen
Production Electrician........James Maloney
Associate Production Electrician........Brad Robertson
Production Properties........Emiliano Pares
Head Properties........Brian Schweppe
Assistant Properties........Michael Critchlow
Production Sound........Phil Lojo,
........Paul DelCioppo
Head Sound........Cassy Givens
Sound Assistant........Gabe Wood
Wardrobe Supervisor........Rick Kelly
Dressers........Jenny Barnes,
........Gary Biangone,
........Franklin Hollenbeck,
........Phillip Rolfe,
........Keith Shaw,
........Franc Weinperl

Hair Supervisor........Frederick Waggoner
Hairdresser........Amanda Duffy
Associate Music Director........Steven Malone
Additional Orchestrations........Steve Margoshes,
........Dave Siegel
Music Preparation........Anixter Rice Music Services
Electronic Music Programming........Jeff Marder
Associate to Mr.Menken........Rick Kunis
Assistant to John Miller........Jennifer Coolbaugh
Rehearsal Musicians........Paul Davis,
........Mat Eisenstein
Music Production Assistant........Brendan Whiting
Dialect & Vocal Coach........Shane Ann Younts
Assistant to Mr.Calhoun........Derek Hersey
Children's Guardian........Vanessa Brown
Children's Tutoring........On Location Education/
........Nancy Van Ness,
........Beverly Brennan
Physical Therapy........PhysioArts

ORCHESTRA
Conductor........Mark Hummel
Associate Conductor........Steven Malone
Assistant Conductor........Mat Eisenstein

Woodwinds: Tom Murray, Mark Thrasher; Trumpet/Flugel: Trevor D. Neumann; Trombone: Dan Levine; Guitar: Brian Koonin; Bass: Ray Kilday; Drums: Paul Davis; Percussion: Ed Shea; Keyboards: Mat Eisenstein, Steven Malone; Violin: Mary Rowell; Cello: Deborah Assael-Migliore

Music Coordinator: John Miller

TELSEY + COMPANY CASTING
Bernie Telsey CSA, Will Cantler CSA, David Vaccari CSA, Bethany Knox CSA, Craig Burns CSA, Tiffany Little Canfield CSA, Rachel Hoffman CSA, Justin Huff CSA, Patrick Goodwin CSA, Abbie Brady-Dalton CSA, David Morris, Cesar A. Rocha, Andrew Femenella, Karyn Casi, Kristina Bramhall, Jessie Malone

Advertising........Serino Coyne, Inc.
Production Photography........Deen Van Meer
Production Travel........Jill L. Citron
Payroll Managers........Anthony DeLuca,
........Cathy Guerra
Corporate Counsel........Michael Rosenfeld

CREDITS
Custom scenery and automation by Hudson Scenic Studio, Inc. Lighting equipment by Production Resource Group, LLC. Sound equipment by Masque Sound. Video projection system provided by Scharff Weisberg, Inc. Soft goods by iWeiss. Costumes by Carelli Costumes, Jennifer Love Studios, Claudia Diaz Costumes. Millinery by Rodney Gordon. Shoes by JC Theatrical & Custom Footwear Inc.; T.O. Dey; Capezio. Rehearsal sets by Proof Productions, Inc. Ricola cough drops courtesy of Ricola USA, Inc.

NEWSIES originally premiered at Paper Mill Playhouse, Milburn, New Jersey. NEWSIES rehearsed at the New 42nd Street Studios & Ripley Grier Studios

Disney Theatrical Productions

President....................Thomas Schumacher
EVP & Managing Director....................David Schrader
Senior Vice President, International....................Ron Kollen
Vice President, International, Europe....................Fiona Thomas
Vice President, International, Australia....................James Thane
Vice President, Operations....................Dana Amendola
Vice President, Publicity....................Joe Quenqua
Vice President, Domestic....................Jack Eldon
Vice President, Human Resources....................June Heindel
Director, Domestic Touring....................Michael Buchanan
Director, Worldwide Publicity....................Michael Cohen
Director, Regional Engagements....................Scott A. Hemerling
Director, Regional Engagements....................Kelli Palan
Director, Regional Engagements....................Deborah Warren
Manager, Domestic Touring & Planning....................Liz Botros
Manager, Human Resources....................Jewel Neal
Manager, Publicity....................Lindsay Braverman
Project Manager....................Ryan Pears
Senior Computer Support Analyst....................Kevin A. McGuire
IT/Business Analyst....................William Boudiette

Creative & Production
Executive Music Producer....................Chris Montan
VP, Creative Development....................Steve Fickinger
VP, Production....................Anne Quart
Director, International Production....................Felipe Gamba
Director, Labor Relations....................Edward Lieber
Associate Director....................Jeff Lee
Production Supervisor....................Clifford Schwartz
Production Manager....................Eduardo Castro
Manager, Labor Relations....................Stephanie Cheek
Manager, Physical Production....................Karl Chmielewski
Manager, Creative Development....................Jane Abramson
Manager, Theatrical Licensing....................David R. Scott
Dramaturg & Literary Manager....................Ken Cerniglia
Manager, Education Outreach....................Lisa Mitchell

Marketing
Senior Vice President....................Andrew Flatt
Director, Creative Resources....................Victor Adams
Director, Synergy & Partnership....................Kevin Banks
Director, Digital Marketing....................Kyle Young
Design Manager....................James Anderer
Manager, Media & Strategy....................Jared Comess
Manager, Creative Services....................Lauren Daghini
Manager, Synergy & Partnership....................Sarah Schlesinger
Manager, Consumer Insights....................Craig Trachtenberg
Manager, Digital Marketing....................Peter Tulba

Sales
Vice President, National Sales....................Bryan Dockett
National Sales Manager....................Victoria Cairl
Sr. Manager, Sales & Ticketing....................Nick Falzon
Manager, Group Sales....................Hunter Robertson

Business and Legal Affairs
Senior Vice President....................Jonathan Olson
Director....................Daniel M. Posener
Director....................Seth Stuhl
Sr. Paralegal....................Jessica White

Finance
VP, Finance/Business Development....................Mario Iannetta
Director, Finance....................Joe McClafferty
Director, Business Development....................Michael Barra
Director, Accounting....................Leena Matthew
Manager, Finance....................Liz Jurist Schwarzwalder
Manager, Production Accounting....................Nick Judge
Manager, Accounting....................Adrineh Ghoukassian
Senior Business Analyst....................Sven Rittershaus
Senior Financial Analyst....................Mikhail Medvedev
Senior Financial Analyst....................Jason Ve
Senior Business Planner....................Jennifer August
Production Accountant....................Joy Sims Brown
Production Accountant....................Angela DiSanti
Assistant Production Accountant....................Isander Rojas

Administrative Staff
Brian Bahr, Sarah Bills, Elizabeth Boulger, Whitney Britt, Jonelle Brown, Amy Caldamone, Michael Dei Cas, Preston Copley, Alanna Degner, Britanny Dobbs, Cara Epstein, Nicholas Faranda, Cristi Finn, Phil Grippe, Greg Josken, Cyntia Leo, Colleen McCormack, Brendan Padgett, Matt Quinones, Jillian Robbins, Kattia Soriano, Lee Taglin, Anji Taylor

DISNEY THEATRICAL MERCHANDISE
Vice President....................Steven Downing
Merchandise Manager....................Neil Markman
District Manager....................Alyssa Somers
Associate Buyer....................Violet Burlaza
Assistant Manager, Inventory....................Suzanne Jakel
On-Site Retail Manager....................Jeff Knizer
On-Site Assistant Retail Manager....................Jana Cristiano

SPECIAL THANKS
James M. Nederlander, James L. Nederlander, Nick Scandalios, the Nederlander organization, TDF Costume Collection, Paper Mill Playhouse, Prop N Spoon, Jake Zerrer.

Disney Theatrical Productions
c/o The New Amsterdam Theatre
214 West 42nd Street
New York, NY 10036
www.disneyonbroadway.com

For information address Disney Editions,
1101 Flower Street, Glendale, California 91201

Produced by Welcome Enterprises, Inc.
6 West 18th Street, New York, New York 10011
Project Director & Designer: H. Clark Wakabayashi

ISBN 978-1-4847-0451-6

V424-9091-2-13214
Printed in South Korea
First Edition
10 9 8 7 6 5 4 3 2 1

Visit www.disneybooks.com
Visit www.disneyonbroadway.com

PHOTO CREDITS:

pp.2–3, 4, 6, 7, 9, 50, 54–55, 58, 62–63, 67, 71A, 73, 74–75, 77, 78, 80, 84, 86, 87, 88, 92, 95, 99, 100, 113, 116, 122D, 131B, 132B, 146 by Deen Van Meer; pp.70A, 82, 104, 108–109, 120, 122F, 123C, 123G, 131A by Heidi Gutman; pp.10, 13, 14, 15, 16B, 21, 66A by Lewis Hine; pp.11, 25, 41, 51, 60–61, 93, 117, 136, 147 by Sven Ortel; p.12 by G.W. Bromley; pp.16A, 19B courtesy of the Library of Congress; p.18A by H.J. Myers; p.18B by Purdy; p.19A courtesy of Corbis; p.20A courtesy of New York City Centennial Classroom; p.20B courtesy of Rare Books & Manuscript Library, Yale University; pp.24, 27, 30, 32, 34 by Andrew Cooper; p.26 courtesy of Bob Tzudiker & Noni White; p.33 by Emily Powell; p.35 courtesy of Disney Photo Archive; p.38C courtesy of Michael Fatica; p.40 by Detroit Publishing Company; p.42 by Carol Rosegg; p.43 by Alan Menken; p.52 by Kevin Sprague; pp.53A, 53B, 56, 57A by Tobin Ost; pp.57B, 60, 64, 65A, 112 by T. Clark Erickson; p.59 by Mark Stys; p.65B by Jeff Croiter; pp.66B, 68–69 by Jess Goldstein; pp.70B, 76, 83, 97, 102–103, 105, 106, 123A, 123B by Eduardo Castro; p.71B courtesy of the *Wall Street Journal*; pp.72, 81 by Jerry Dalia; p.94 courtesy of Andrew Keenan–Bolger; p.101 courtesy of ABC; p.107 by Preston Copley; pp.106, 110A, 111A, 122A, 123D, 130, 134, 135, 139, 143, 154–155 by Timothy Eaker; pp.110B, 111B by Anita and Steve Shevett; pp. 118, 119, 121 courtesy of DTG Marketing Department; pp.124, 125A, 125B courtesy of DTG Merchandise Department; p.125C courtesy of Luke Camp; pp.126–127 by Matthew Murphy; p.129 by Colleen McCormack; p.132A courtesy of Brendon Stimson; p.133 by Adam Taylor; p.137 Mark Ashman; pp.122G, 138 Lorenzo Bevialaqua; p.140A courtesy of Matthew Schechter; pp.140B, 141 courtesy of Jake Lucas; p.123F by Greg Josken; p.122B by James Anderer; p.123E by Paul Chase; p.122C courtesy of Nicholas Lampiasi; p.122E courtesy of Mark Aldrich

FANSIE PHOTOS COURTESY OF:

Daniela Diaz Jarquin (22), Meghan Brown (22), Brenna Corporal (22), Laura McVey (22), Amy Manske (22), Torey Sorel (22), Gabriella Trentacoste (23), Jeanette Logan (23), Ivan Joshua (23), Allison Wagner (23), Kara Hynes (23), Darlene Slavick (38), Shannon Prendergast (38), Jessica Sininger (38), Ben Southerland (38), Kate Reitz (38), Megan Robison (39), Hannah Moors (39), David Jacobs (39), Sarah Mariette (39), Megan O'Neill (48), Megan Clancy (48), Tess McDermott (48), Erin Elliott (48), Aimee Weyrauch (48), Ashley Carpenter (48), Jennifer Sothy (49), Keely O'Connor (49), Kayla Follett (49), Heather O (49), Rebecca Pruitt (49), Hope Dancy (89), Jonah Robinson (90), Alexa Reyes (90), Jessica Gleason (90), Melanie Cleveland (90), Rachel Green (90), Liz Hornbach (90), Erika Panzarino (90), Clara Kennedy (91), Christine Mantineo (91), Hannah Stengele (91), Carly Palmatier (91), Wendi Reichstein (107), Katie Carbone (114), Kim Buchly (114), Mackenzie Aladjem (114), Samantha Shoop (114), Rosanna Pagtakhan (114), Dana Sevean (114), Amanda Croke (115), Melissa Rhees (115), Carolyn Tomlinson (115), Alex Bishop (115), Amanda McKenzie (115), Aislinn Keenan (120), Marissa Scarangella (144), Cassidy Shuflin (144), Julia Simoes de Oliveira (144), Marisa Pittarelli (144), Rebecca Bailey (144), Nate Patrick Siebert (144), Lindsey Halwachs (145), Erica Redmond (145), Emily Hornburg (145), Marissa Casano (145), Tommy Faircloth (145)